Walking in Grace and Glory

Other Books by David Roper

The God Who Walks Beside Us
In Quietness and Confidence
Psalm 23
Seeing God
The Strength of a Man

Walking in Grace and Glory

90 DAYS IN THE PSALMS

David Roper

Scripture quotations, unless otherwise indicated, are taken from the Holy Bible, New International Version®, NIV®. Copyright © 1973, 1978, 1984, 2011 by Biblica, Inc.™ Used by permission of Zondervan. All rights reserved worldwide. www.zondervan.com.

Scripture quotations marked ESV are taken from the ESV® Bible (The Holy Bible, English Standard Version®), copyright © 2001 by Crossway, a publishing ministry of Good News Publishers. Used by permission. All rights reserved.

Scripture quotations marked NKJV are from the New King James Version®. Copyright © 1982 by Thomas Nelson. Used by permission. All rights reserved.

Scripture quotations marked NLT are taken from the Holy Bible, New Living Translation, copyright © 1996, 2004, 2015 by Tyndale House Foundation. Used by permission of Tyndale House Publishers, Inc., Carol Stream, Illinois 60188. All rights reserved.

Interior design by Beth Shagene

Library of Congress Cataloging-in-Publication Data Available
ISBN: 978-1-64070-036-9

Printed in the United States of America
21 22 23 24 25 26 27 28 29 / 9 8 7 6 5 4 3 2 1

Contents

Foreword

David Roper never fashioned himself a writer. Nor a pastor, for that matter.

After graduating from seminary in his native Texas, he anticipated spending his years in camping ministry. Yet his words—both written and spoken—have touched the lives of people across the globe, and in our shared hometown of Boise, Idaho. His *The Strength of a Man* was born from a series of one-page notes written for friends who gathered with him at local eateries each Wednesday morning for breakfast and study.

From those humble beginnings has poured a steady stream of wisdom shared through *Our Daily Bread* for nearly twenty years, written with the same genuine, caring motivation as his Wednesday notes: to encourage us, his fellow sojourners. David begins each morning in his wood-paneled study, immersing himself in God's Word, in prayer, and in the writings of favorite authors such as C. S. Lewis, Peter Kreeft, and George MacDonald. He knows that one can only give what one already possesses, and he earnestly desires to give readers more of the Lord he loves: "The more we receive, the more we have to give" (*In Quietness and Confidence*, p. 102). The abundance of what he's shared with us over a lifetime of writing is testament to all he's received from God in those quiet morning hours.

David's wisdom imparted to me as a fellow writer was similar: "Fill yourself full of God and write out of that reservoir of truth. Write out of your love for Him and His for you." Those words called to my mind one of Idaho's greatest natural treasures: Lake Pend Oreille. It is known not just for the beauty of the surrounding forests and for sustaining an abundance of wildlife both in and around its waters but for being one of the largest and deepest lakes in the western part of the United States. It's the kind of place outdoorsman and angler David Roper often uses to illustrate truths about God in his writing. "Nature," he once wrote, "is never wasted. It daily displays the truth, goodness, and beauty of the One who brought it into being."

Lake Pend Oreille—French for "ear hanging"—is so named because the lake is shaped like an ear when viewed from above. I like to think of it as being upturned to hear God's wisdom from on high. Through David's invitations in the daily readings bound here, may we turn our ears upward with anticipation that God still speaks to the hearts of men and women. If we listen well, we too might become beautiful, deep reservoirs of Truth—offering life to those around us.

—Kirsten Holmberg
Our Daily Bread Writer
Boise, Idaho

I removed the burden from their shoulders;
their hands were set free from the basket.
In your distress you called and I rescued you,
I answered you out of a thundercloud;
I tested you at the waters of Meribah.
Hear me, my people, and I will warn you—
if you would only listen to me, Israel!
You shall have no foreign god among you;
you shall not worship any god other than me.
I am the Lord your God,
who brought you up out of Egypt.
Open wide your mouth and I will fill it.

When God Thunders

You called in trouble, and I delivered you;
I answered you in the secret place of thunder;
I tested you at the waters of Meribah. Selah.
—PSALM 81:7 (NKJV)

Thunder rolls across the Sawtooth Mountains, crashing and echoing through the peaks and canyons, shaking the ground with celestial sonic booms. My old dog cuts and runs. I stand amazed and delighted.

The storm reminds me of the "secret place of thunder" from which God answered His people (Psalm 81:7). Israel cried out from the straw pits and brick kilns of Egypt. In time, God's salvation rolled over the land in peals of thunder (Exodus 9:13–34).

Another Psalm speaks of the storm that overshadowed the Israelites as they passed through the Red Sea (Psalm 77:16–20). Its thunder spelled doom for the Egyptians but deliverance to God's people. Each resounding clap was the comforting voice of a Father speaking to His children.

When Jesus foretold His death in John 12:28–29, He called on His Father to glorify His name. A voice answered from heaven saying, "I have glorified it, and will glorify it again." To the crowd, it sounded like thunder.

Are you in trouble? Cry out to God in your sorrow and distress. You may not hear the thunder roll, but His voice will reverberate through the heavens once more as He answers you "in the secret place of thunder." God will speak comfort to your heart and deliver you from your fears.

Those who trust in God
find comfort in His power.

My heart is in anguish within me;
the terrors of death have fallen on me.
Fear and trembling have beset me;
horror has overwhelmed me.
I said, "Oh, that I had the wings of a dove!
I would fly away and be at rest.
I would flee far away
and stay in the desert;
I would hurry to my place of shelter,
far from the tempest and storm."
Lord, confuse the wicked, confound their words,
for I see violence and strife in the city.
Day and night they prowl about on its walls;
malice and abuse are within it.
Destructive forces are at work in the city;
threats and lies never leave its streets.
If an enemy were insulting me,
I could endure it;
if a foe were rising against me,
I could hide.
But it is you, a man like myself,
my companion, my close friend,
with whom I once enjoyed sweet fellowship
at the house of God,
as we walked about
among the worshipers.
Let death take my enemies by surprise;
let them go down alive to the realm of the dead,
for evil finds lodging among them.

continued . . .

As for me, I call to God,
and the LORD saves me.
Evening, morning and noon
I cry out in distress,
and he hears my voice.
He rescues me unharmed
from the battle waged against me,
even though many oppose me.
God, who is enthroned from of old,
who does not change—
he will hear them and humble them,
because they have no fear of God.
My companion attacks his friends;
he violates his covenant.
His talk is smooth as butter,
yet war is in his heart;
his words are more soothing than oil,
yet they are drawn swords.
Cast your cares on the LORD
and he will sustain you;
he will never let
the righteous be shaken.

Wings Like a Dove

"Oh, that I had wings like a dove!
I would fly away and be at rest."
—PSALM 55:6 (NKJV)

David sighed, "Oh, that I had wings like a dove! I would fly away and be at rest" (Psalm 55:6). As for me, I'd build a cabin in the Sawtooths, or I'd take a permanent post in a fire-lookout tower. When life weighs on me, I too yearn to fly away and be at rest.

David wrote freely about his circumstances: Violence, oppression, and strife surrounded him on all sides, stirred up by the disloyalty of an old friend (55:8–14). Fear and terror, pain and trembling, anxiety and restlessness overwhelmed him (vv. 4–5). Is it any wonder he longed to fly away?

But escape was impossible. He could not evade his lot. He could only give his circumstances to God: "As for me, I call to God, and the LORD saves me. Evening, morning and noon I cry out in distress, and he hears my voice" (vv. 16–17).

Whatever our circumstances—a burdensome ministry, a difficult marriage, joblessness, or a deep loneliness—we can give them to God. He has lifted the burden of our sins; will He not lift the weight of our sorrows? We have trusted Him with our eternal souls; can we not entrust our present circumstances to Him? "Cast your cares on the LORD and he will sustain you" (55:22).

**Because God cares about us,
we can leave our cares with Him.**

Oh, how I love your law!
I meditate on it all day long.
Your commands are always with me
and make me wiser than my enemies.
I have more insight than all my teachers,
for I meditate on your statutes.
I have more understanding than the elders,
for I obey your precepts.
I have kept my feet from every evil path
so that I might obey your word.
I have not departed from your laws,
for you yourself have taught me.
How sweet are your words to my taste,
sweeter than honey to my mouth!
I gain understanding from your precepts;
therefore I hate every wrong path.

Initial Point

Jesus answered, "It is written:
'Man shall not live on bread alone,
but on every word that comes
from the mouth of God.'"
—MATTHEW 4:4

If you drive south of our home in Boise, Idaho, you'll see a volcanic butte that rises out of the sagebrush on the east side of the road. This is the initial point from which the state of Idaho was surveyed.

In 1867, four years after Idaho was organized as a territory, Lafayette Cartee, the Surveyor General of the United States, commissioned Peter Bell to survey the new territory. Bell took a sledge and drove a brass post into a little knob on the summit of that butte, declaring it to be the initial point from which he began his survey.

The survey established the language of land description in Idaho: Townships are designated north and south of the initial point; ranges are designated east and west. With such descriptions, you always know exactly where you are.

We may read many books, but the Word of God is our "initial point," the fixed reference point. John Wesley read widely, but he always referred to himself as "a man of one book." Nothing can compare to the Book of books, the Word of God. When we allow the Bible to be our guide in all of life, we can say with the psalmist, "How sweet are your words to my taste, sweeter than honey to my mouth!" (Psalm 119:103).

Dear Lord, we are grateful for your Book. In it we learn of you and find guidance and direction for our lives. Help us to learn to love your Word and to eagerly dig into its pages. Amen.

The Bible is like a compass:
if followed, you're going in the right direction.

Unless the LORD builds the house,
the builders labor in vain.
Unless the LORD watches over the city,
the guards stand watch in vain.
In vain you rise early
and stay up late,
toiling for food to eat—
for he grants sleep to those he loves.
Children are a heritage from the LORD,
offspring a reward from him.
Like arrows in the hands of a warrior
are children born in one's youth.
Blessed is the man
whose quiver is full of them.
They will not be put to shame
when they contend with their opponents in court.

Fine Crystal

Children are a heritage from the LORD,
offspring a reward from him.
—PSALM 127:3

I have a friend—call her "Mary"—who tells me that her fondest memory is of the morning she broke her mother's "priceless" crystal.

Mary's mother was having a party. She had taken her fine crystal from the cupboard and carefully washed it and placed it on the table. The crystal represented the only valuable material possession her mother owned, and it was used only on special occasions.

In her rush to get things ready for her guests, Mary's mother said to her young daughter, "Would you please find some place that's not underfoot?" So Mary crawled underneath the table. Unfortunately, she kicked the leg of the table and the crystal crashed to the floor. "Crystal exploded like shrapnel," she recalls. She had destroyed the most elegant thing her mother possessed.

"I'm so sorry," the little girl sobbed. Her mother gathered her in her arms and whispered, "Don't cry, honey. You are far more valuable to me than mere crystal."

Children are indeed our most valuable possession, more precious than anything we could ever buy or earn. They are "a heritage from the LORD" and "a reward" (Psalm 127:3).

Do your children know how precious they are to you? Why not tell them today?

**Little children are
of great value to God.**

Now this I know:
The LORD gives victory to his anointed.
He answers him from his heavenly sanctuary
with the victorious power of his right hand.
Some trust in chariots and some in horses,
but we trust in the name of the LORD our God.
They are brought to their knees and fall,
but we rise up and stand firm.
LORD, give victory to the king!
Answer us when we call!

What's Your Passion?

Some trust in chariots
and some in horses,
but we trust in the name
of the LORD *our God.*
—PSALM 20:7

One of the tellers at my bank has a photograph of a Shelby Cobra roadster on his window. (The Cobra is a high-performance automobile originally built by the Ford Motor Company.)

One day, while transacting business at the bank, I asked him if that was his car. "No," he replied, "that's my passion, my reason to get up every morning and go to work. I'm going to own one someday."

I understand this young man's passion. A friend of mine owned a Cobra, and I drove it on one occasion! It's a mean machine! But a Cobra, like everything else in this world, isn't worth living for. Those who trust in things apart from God "are brought to their knees and fall," according to the psalmist (Psalm 20:8).

That's because we were made for God and nothing else will do—a truth we validate in our experience every day: We buy this or that because we think these things will make us happy, but like a child receiving a dozen Christmas presents or more, we ask ourselves, "Is this all?" Something is always missing.

Nothing this world has to offer us—even very good things—fully satisfies us. There is a measure of enjoyment in them, but our happiness soon fades away (1 John 2:17). Indeed, "God cannot give us happiness and peace apart from Himself," C. S. Lewis concluded. "There is no such thing."

> **There is a longing in every heart**
> **that only Jesus can satisfy.**

Blessed are those who have regard for the weak;
the LORD delivers them in times of trouble.
The LORD protects and preserves them—
they are counted among the blessed in the land—
he does not give them over to the desire of their foes.
The LORD sustains them on their sickbed
and restores them from their bed of illness.

Paying Attention

Blessed are those who have regard for the weak;
the LORD delivers them in times of trouble.
—PSALM 41:1

John Newton, the eighteenth-century author of "Amazing Grace," wrote, "If, as I go home, a child has dropped a halfpenny, and if, by giving it another, I can wipe away its tears, I feel I have done something. I should be glad to do greater things; but I will not neglect this."

These days, it's not hard to find someone in need of comfort: A care-worn cashier in a grocery store working a second job to make ends meet; a refugee longing for home; a single mother whose flood of worries has washed away her hope; a lonely old man who fears he has outlived his usefulness.

But what are we to do? "Blessed is he who considers the poor," wrote David (Psalm 41:1 NKJV). Even if we can't alleviate the poverty of those we meet along the way, we can consider them—a verb that means "to pay attention."

We can let people know we care. We can treat them with courtesy and respect, though they may be testy or tiresome. We can listen with interest to their stories. And we can pray for them or with them—the most helpful and healing act of all.

Remember the old paradox Jesus gave us when He said, "It is more blessed to give than to receive" (Acts 20:35). Paying attention pays off, for we're happiest when we give ourselves away. Consider the poor.

Father, as we go through our day, show us the everyday folks who need our attention. Grant us the love and the patience to truly consider them, as you have so patiently loved us.

Only a life given away for love's sake
is worth living.
—FREDERICK BUECHNER

PSALM 8:1–2

Lord, our Lord,
how majestic is your name in all the earth!
You have set your glory
in the heavens.
Through the praise of children and infants
you have established a stronghold against your enemies,
to silence the foe and the avenger.

Out of the Mouths of Babes

Through the praise of children and infants
you have established a stronghold
against your enemies,
to silence the foe and the avenger.
—PSALM 8:2

Psalm 8 begins with a startling contrast. David seems to suggest that while God has revealed His glory in the skies, another persuasive answer to His critics comes in the utterances of a child: "Through the praise of children and infants you have established a stronghold against your enemies, to silence the foe and the avenger" (v. 2).

Why is a child's praise so persuasive? For one thing, it's because, unlike the impersonal universe, a child can know and love God.

Jesus quoted Psalm 8:2 when religious leaders were scandalized that children were running around in the temple shouting, "Hosanna to the Son of David!" (Matthew 21:15–16). These little ones knew—as those leaders did not know—that Jesus was the long-awaited Son of God.

Some of my most memorable moments as a parent came when I knelt beside our children's beds at night, and they opened their hearts to God. The simplicity of their love and trust as they prayed touched me deeply, dispelled my doubts and fears, and drew me to faith.

We must never take lightly little ones who believe in Christ (Matthew 18:6, 10). Their witness is great, as is the witness in the skies.

Children are God's precious jewels
—help them shine for Christ.

The heavens declare the glory of God;
the skies proclaim the work of his hands.
Day after day they pour forth speech;
night after night they reveal knowledge.
They have no speech, they use no words;
no sound is heard from them.
Yet their voice goes out into all the earth,
their words to the ends of the world.
In the heavens God has pitched a tent for the sun.
It is like a bridegroom coming out of his chamber,
like a champion rejoicing to run his course.
It rises at one end of the heavens
and makes its circuit to the other;
nothing is deprived of its warmth.

Why Is There Color?

*The heavens declare the glory of God;
the skies proclaim the work of his hands.*
—PSALM 19:1

Why do some trees turn into a collage of radiant maroon, red, orange, and yellow colors in the fall? Trees are green in the summer because chlorophyll, a green pigment in the leaves, absorbs red and blue light from the sun. The light reflected from the leaves appears green to our eyes.

Chlorophyll is an unstable substance, and bright sunlight causes it to decompose rapidly. Therefore, plants must continuously synthesize and regenerate it. The shortening days and cool nights of autumn, however, interfere with this process. As chlorophyll breaks down, the green colors of the leaves begin to fade. Some trees change from green to bright yellow as the chlorophyll degrades. In others, the action of sugar in the leaves creates a red pigment, causing the leaves to turn maroon, purple, and bright red as the chlorophyll fades.

But why do we have color? It seems to serve no practical purpose—at least none that scientists can discern. And why are there photoreceptors in our eyes that enable us to see it?

I believe that God's goodness is the point of His creation. He is "good to all; he has compassion on all he has made" (Psalm 145:9). He colored the world for our childlike delight. He's like that, you know.

**God's glory shines
through His creation.**

I will praise you more and more.
My mouth will tell of your righteous deeds,
of your saving acts all day long—
though I know not how to relate them all.
I will come and proclaim your mighty acts, Sovereign LORD;
I will proclaim your righteous deeds, yours alone.
Since my youth, God, you have taught me,
and to this day I declare your marvelous deeds.
Even when I am old and gray,
do not forsake me, my God,
till I declare your power to the next generation,
your mighty acts to all who are to come.
Your righteousness, God, reaches to the heavens,
you who have done great things.
Who is like you, God?
Though you have made me see troubles,
many and bitter,
you will restore my life again;
from the depths of the earth
you will again bring me up.
You will increase my honor
and comfort me once more.
I will praise you with the harp
for your faithfulness, my God;
I will sing praise to you with the lyre,
Holy One of Israel.
My lips will shout for joy
when I sing praise to you—
I whom you have delivered.
My tongue will tell of your righteous acts
all day long,
for those who wanted to harm me
have been put to shame and confusion.

Growing Old; Growing Up

Even when I am old and gray,
do not forsake me, my God,
till I declare your power to the next generation,
your mighty acts to all who are to come.
—PSALM 71:18

Old age is the season when we can give ourselves to "soul-making," as the Quakers say. We can concentrate on getting to know God better and cultivating character traits that make us more like Him. Age breaks down our strength and energy and strips us of our busyness. It's God's way of getting us to slow down so we'll take more time for Him. We can think more deeply about life, about ourselves, and about others.

Change is an inevitable part of life. We're being shaped every minute we live. Every thought, every decision, every action, every emotion, every response is shaping us into one kind of person or another. Either we're moving toward likeness to Christ or away from Him into some sort of caricature of the person God intended us to be.

It's true, we lose some things as we age: physical strength, quickness, agility. But think of the calm God gives us, the peace He leaves us, the benefits of His salvation, and His faithfulness to us (Psalm 71:15).

Old age is the best time to grow in grace and godliness, in inner strength and beauty of character. "The silver-haired head," the wise man said, "is a crown of glory, if it is found in the way of righteousness" (Proverbs 16:31 NKJV).

> "Grow up" is what the young are told—
> "age gracefully" when growing old.

Deliver me from my enemies, O God;
be my fortress against those who are attacking me.
Deliver me from evildoers
and save me from those who are after my blood.
See how they lie in wait for me!
Fierce men conspire against me
for no offense or sin of mine, LORD.
I have done no wrong, yet they are ready to attack me.
Arise to help me; look on my plight!
You, LORD God Almighty,
you who are the God of Israel,
rouse yourself to punish all the nations;
show no mercy to wicked traitors. . . .
But I will sing of your strength,
in the morning I will sing of your love;
for you are my fortress,
my refuge in times of trouble.
You are my strength, I sing praise to you;
you, God, are my fortress,
my God on whom I can rely.

Snapping, Snarling Thoughts

You are my fortress,
my refuge in times my trouble.
—PSALM 59:16

Many years ago, my father and I hiked through Big Bend in Texas. It's a national park now, but in those days it was rough country.

One night we were rolling out our sleeping bags when a couple with a dog asked if they could camp nearby. We welcomed their company and turned in for the night. They tethered their dog to a stake beside their tent.

Some hours later my father nudged me awake and turned his flashlight into the darkness. Illuminated by the light, we saw pairs of yellow eyes peering out of the shadows. A pack of snapping and snarling coyotes were closing in on the dog. Although we chased them off and our neighbors put the dog in their tent, we slept fitfully.

I think of that night when I read Psalm 59 and David's twice-repeated imagery: "They return at evening, snarling like dogs, and prowl about the city" (vv. 6, 14). David was thinking of Saul's army that was closing in on him. I think, however, of the thoughts that return to menace us. They come back at nightfall, snapping and snarling: "You're stupid." "You're a failure." "You're useless." "Who needs you?"

When we have such thoughts, we can revel in God's unconditional, unending love. His steady devotion is our refuge in the dark night of self-doubt and fear (v. 16).

Knowing that God loves us
can dispel doubt.

LORD, you have seen this; do not be silent.
Do not be far from me, Lord.
Awake, and rise to my defense!
Contend for me, my God and Lord.
Vindicate me in your righteousness, LORD my God;
do not let them gloat over me.
Do not let them think, "Aha, just what we wanted!"
or say, "We have swallowed him up."
May all who gloat over my distress
be put to shame and confusion;
may all who exalt themselves over me
be clothed with shame and disgrace.
May those who delight in my vindication
shout for joy and gladness;
may they always say, "The LORD be exalted,
who delights in the well-being of his servant."
My tongue will proclaim your righteousness,
your praises all day long.

The Salt Lick

May those who delight in my vindication
shout for joy and gladness;
may they always say, "The LORD be exalted,
who delights in the well-being of his servant."
—PSALM 35:27

One spring I put a salt block in the bushes a few yards behind my mountain home. I was hoping to draw in a small herd of deer that grazed at a distance. Each morning I slowly opened the window shades, hoping to see deer gathered around the lick; each morning I was disappointed. I didn't think the herd would ever find the salt.

Then one morning as I drew the shades, to my utter delight I spied a magnificent, young buck. He was licking the block, oblivious to my presence. I stood there for a long time watching him and savoring my joy.

My wife Carolyn reminded me later in the day that God takes a similar joy in me. The psalmist said that the Lord "delights in the well-being of his servant" (Psalm 35:27). He delights in bringing good to me and in seeing me enjoy His blessings.

English preacher John Owen (1616–1683) said, "The souls of the saints are the garden of Jesus Christ, . . . a garden for delight; He rejoices in them."

We may encounter people who want to hurt us and gloat over our distress, but not our Lord (vv. 25–27). He longs to be good to us, to satisfy our deepest longings with His love. We are His heart's delight.

**God takes delight in us—
how can we help but delight in Him!**

PSALM 100

Shout for joy to the LORD, all the earth.
Worship the LORD with gladness;
come before him with joyful songs.
Know that the LORD is God.
It is he who made us, and we are his;
we are his people, the sheep of his pasture.
Enter his gates with thanksgiving
and his courts with praise;
give thanks to him and praise his name.
For the LORD is good and his love endures forever;
his faithfulness continues through all generations.

You're an Original

Know that the LORD is God.
It is he who made us, and we are his.
—PSALM 100:3

Each of us is an original from God's hand. There are no self-made men or women. No one ever became talented, buffed, or bright all by himself or herself. God made each of us all by himself. He thought of us and formed us out of His unspeakable love.

God made your body, mind, and soul. And He isn't done with you; He is still making you. His single-minded purpose is our maturity: "He who began a good work in you will carry it on to completion until the day of Christ Jesus" (Philippians 1:6). God is making you braver, stronger, purer, more peaceful, more loving, less selfish—the kind of person you've perhaps always wanted to be.

"[God's] unfailing love continues forever, and his faithfulness continues to each generation" (Psalm 100:5 NLT). God has always loved you ("forever" goes both ways), and He will be faithful to you to the end.

You've been given a love that lasts forever and a God who will never give up on you. That's a good reason to have joy and to "come before him with joyful songs"! (v. 2).

If you can't carry a tune, just give Him a shout-out: "Shout for joy to the LORD" (v. 1).

**Spiritual growth occurs
when faith is cultivated.**

Give thanks to the LORD, for he is good.
His love endures forever.
Give thanks to the God of gods.
His love endures forever.
Give thanks to the Lord of lords:
His love endures forever.
to him who alone does great wonders,
His love endures forever.
who by his understanding made the heavens,
His love endures forever.
who spread out the earth upon the waters,
His love endures forever.
who made the great lights—
His love endures forever.
the sun to govern the day,
His love endures forever.
the moon and stars to govern the night;
His love endures forever.

Desert Solitaire

The land produced vegetation:
plants bearing seed according to
their kinds and trees bearing fruit
with seed in it according to their kinds.
And God saw that it was good.
—GENESIS 1:12

Desert Solitaire is Edward Abbey's personal history of his summers as a park ranger in what is now called Arches National Park in Utah. The book is worth reading if only for Abbey's bright language and vivid descriptions of the US Southwest.

But Abbey, for all his artistry, was an atheist who could see nothing beyond the surface of the beauty he enjoyed. How sad! He lived his entire life in praise of beauty and missed the point of it all.

Most ancient peoples had theories of origins enshrouded in legend, myth, and song. But Israel's story of creation was unique: It told of a God who created beauty for our enjoyment and childlike delight. God thought up the cosmos, spoke it into being and pronounced it "beautiful." (The Hebrew word for *good* also signifies "beauty.") Then, having created a paradise, God in love spoke us into being, placed us in Eden, and told us, "Enjoy!"

Some see and enjoy the beauty of the Creator's good gifts all around them but don't "worship him as God or even give him thanks." They "think up foolish ideas of what God [is] like. As a result, their minds [become] dark and confused" (Romans 1:21 NLT).

Others see beauty, say, "Thank you, God," and step into His light.

All of creation reflects
the beauty of God.

Where can I go from your Spirit?
Where can I flee from your presence?
If I go up to the heavens, you are there;
if I make my bed in the depths, you are there.
If I rise on the wings of the dawn,
if I settle on the far side of the sea,
even there your hand will guide me,
your right hand will hold me fast.
If I say, "Surely the darkness will hide me
and the light become night around me,"
even the darkness will not be dark to you;
the night will shine like the day,
for darkness is as light to you.

Reaching Out
in the Darkness

The night will shine like the day,
for darkness is as light to you.
—PSALM 139:12

Our old dog—a West Highland White Terrier—sleeps curled up at the foot of our bed. That's been her place for thirteen years.

Normally she doesn't move or make a sound, but lately she's been pawing us gently in the middle of the night. At first we thought she wanted to go outside, so we tried to accommodate her. But we realized she just wants to know we are there. She's nearly deaf and partially blind now. She can't see in the darkness and can't hear us move or breathe. Naturally, she gets confused and reaches out for reassurance. So I just reach down and pat her on the head to assure her that I'm there. That's all she wants to know. She takes a turn or two, settles down, and goes back to sleep.

"Where can I flee from Your presence?" David asked God (Psalm 139:7 NKJV). David took this as an immense comfort: "If I settle on the far side of the sea, even there your hand will guide me," he noted. "Even the darkness will not be dark to you" (vv. 9–12).

Lost in darkness? Grieving, fearful, guilty, doubting, discouraged? Not sure of God? The darkness is not dark to Him. Though unseen, He is at hand. He has said, "Never will I leave you; never will I forsake you" (Hebrews 13:5). Reach out your hand for His. He is there.

Dark fears flee in the light
of God's presence.

LORD, hear my prayer,
listen to my cry for mercy;
in your faithfulness and righteousness
come to my relief.
Do not bring your servant into judgment,
for no one living is righteous before you.
The enemy pursues me,
he crushes me to the ground;
he makes me dwell in the darkness
like those long dead.
So my spirit grows faint within me;
my heart within me is dismayed.
I remember the days of long ago;
I meditate on all your works
and consider what your hands have done.
I spread out my hands to you;
I thirst for you like a parched land.

The Good Old Days

I remember the days of long ago;
I meditate on all your works and consider
what your hands have done.
—PSALM 143:5

Sometimes our minds run back through the years and yearn for that better time and place—the "good old days."

But for some, the past harbors only bitter memories. Deep in the night, they ponder their own failures, disillusionments, and fantasies, and think of the cruel hand life has dealt them.

It's better to remember the past as David did by contemplating the good that God has done—to "meditate on all [His] works; . . . consider what [His] hands have done" (Psalm 143:5). As we call to mind the lovingkindness of the Lord, we can see His blessings through the years. These are the memories that foster the highest good. They evoke a deep longing for more of God and more of His tender care. They transform the past into a place of familiarity and fellowship with our Lord.

I heard a story about an elderly woman who would sit in silence for hours in her rocking chair, hands folded in her lap, eyes gazing off into the far distance. One day her daughter asked, "Mother, what do you think about when you sit there so quietly?" Her mother replied softly with a twinkle in her eye, "That's just between Jesus and me."

I pray that our memories and meditations would draw us into His presence.

Fellowship with Christ is
the secret of happiness now and forever.

If you say, "The LORD is my refuge,"
and you make the Most High your dwelling,
no harm will overtake you,
no disaster will come near your tent.
For he will command his angels concerning you
to guard you in all your ways;
they will lift you up in their hands,
so that you will not strike your foot against a stone.
You will tread on the lion and the cobra;
you will trample the great lion and the serpent.
"Because he loves me," says the LORD, "I will rescue him;
I will protect him, for he acknowledges my name.
He will call on me, and I will answer him;
I will be with him in trouble,
I will deliver him and honor him.
With long life I will satisfy him
and show him my salvation."

Snug as a Bug in a Rug!

In peace I will lie down and sleep,
for you alone, LORD,
make me dwell in safety.
—PSALM 4:8

When I was a child, my family lived in a house my father built in the cedar breaks west of Duncanville, Texas. Our house had a small kitchen-dinette area, two bedrooms, and a great room with a large stone fireplace in which we burned two-foot-long cedar logs. That fireplace was the center of warmth in our home.

There were five people in our family: my father and mother, my sister, my cousin, and me. Since we had only two bedrooms, I slept year-round on a porch with canvas screens that rolled down to the floor. Summers were delightful; winters were cold.

I remember dashing from the warmth of the living room onto the porch, tiptoeing across the frost-covered plank floor in my bare feet, leaping into bed and burrowing under a great mountain of blankets. Then, when hail, sleet, or snow lashed our house and the wind howled through the eaves like a pack of wolves, I snuggled down in sheltered rest. "Snug as a bug in a rug," my mother used to say. I doubt that any child ever felt so warm and secure.

Now I know the greatest security of all: God himself. I can "lie down in peace and sleep" (Psalm 4:8 NKJV), knowing that He is my shelter from the stinging storms of life. Enveloped in the warmth of His love, I'm snug as a bug in a rug.

No one is more secure than those
who are in God's hands.

Ascribe to the LORD, you heavenly beings,
ascribe to the LORD glory and strength.
Ascribe to the LORD the glory due his name;
worship the LORD in the splendor of his holiness.
The voice of the LORD is over the waters;
the God of glory thunders,
the LORD thunders over the mighty waters.
The voice of the LORD is powerful;
the voice of the LORD is majestic.
The voice of the LORD breaks the cedars;
the LORD breaks in pieces the cedars of Lebanon.
He makes Lebanon leap like a calf,
Sirion like a young wild ox.
The voice of the LORD strikes
with flashes of lightning.
The voice of the LORD shakes the desert;
the LORD shakes the Desert of Kadesh.
The voice of the LORD twists the oaks
and strips the forests bare.
And in his temple all cry, "Glory!"
The LORD sits enthroned over the flood;
the LORD is enthroned as King forever.
The LORD gives strength to his people;
the LORD blesses his people with peace.

Thunder and Lightning

The voice of the LORD strikes
with flashes of lightning.
—PSALM 29:7

Many years ago, a friend and I were fishing a series of beaver ponds when it started to rain. We took cover under a nearby grove of quaking aspen, but the rain continued to fall. So we decided to call it a day and run for the truck. I had just opened the door when lightning struck the aspen grove with a thunderous fireball that stripped leaves and bark off the trees, leaving a few limbs smoldering. And then there was silence.

We were shaken and awed.

Lightning flashes and thunder rolls across our Idaho valley. I love it—despite my close call. I love the raw power. Voltage! Percussion! Shock and awe! The earth and everything in it trembles and shakes. And then there is peace.

I love lightning and thunder primarily because they are symbols of God's voice (Job 37:4), speaking with stupendous, irresistible power through His Word. "The voice of the LORD strikes with flashes of lightning . . . The LORD gives strength to his people; the LORD blesses his people with peace" (Psalm 29:7, 11). He gives strength to endure, to be patient, to be kind, to sit quietly, to get up and go, to do nothing at all.

May the God of peace be with you.

**Faith connects our weakness
to God's strength.**

PSALM 39

I said, "I will watch my ways
and keep my tongue from sin;
I will put a muzzle on my mouth
while in the presence of the wicked."
So I remained utterly silent,
not even saying anything good.
But my anguish increased;
my heart grew hot within me.
While I meditated, the fire burned;
then I spoke with my tongue:
"Show me, Lord, my life's end
and the number of my days;
let me know how fleeting my life is.
You have made my days a mere handbreadth;
the span of my years is as nothing before you.
Everyone is but a breath,
even those who seem secure.
Surely everyone goes around like a mere phantom;
in vain they rush about, heaping up wealth
without knowing whose it will finally be.

"But now, Lord, what do I look for?
My hope is in you.
Save me from all my transgressions;
do not make me the scorn of fools.
I was silent; I would not open my mouth,
for you are the one who has done this.
Remove your scourge from me;
I am overcome by the blow of your hand.
When you rebuke and discipline anyone for their sin,
you consume their wealth like a moth—
surely everyone is but a breath.
Hear my prayer, LORD,
listen to my cry for help;
do not be deaf to my weeping.
I dwell with you as a foreigner,
a stranger, as all my ancestors were.
Look away from me, that I may enjoy life again
before I depart and am no more."

Traveling Companion

I dwell with you as a foreigner,
a stranger, as all my ancestors were.
—PSALM 39:12

I looked up the members of my seminary graduating class recently and discovered that many of my friends are now deceased. It was a sober reminder of the brevity of life. Seventy years, give or take a few, and we're gone (Psalm 90:10). Israel's poet was right: We're but foreigners here and strangers (39:12).

The brevity of life makes us think about our "end"—the measure of our days and how fleeting they are (v. 4), a feeling that grows more certain as we draw closer to the end of our lives. This world is not our home; we're but visitors on a journey.

Yet we are not alone on the journey. We are foreigners and strangers with God (39:12), a thought that makes the journey less troubling, less frightening, less worrisome. We pass through this world and into the next with a loving Father as our constant companion and guide. We're strangers here on earth, but we are never alone on the journey (73:23–24). We have One who says, "I am with you always" (Matthew 28:20).

We may lose sight of father, mother, spouse, and friends, but we always know that God is walking beside us. An old saying puts it like this: "Good company on the road makes the way to seem lighter."

> As you travel life's weary road,
> let Jesus lift your heavy load.

The Lord is my light and my salvation—
whom shall I fear?
The Lord is the stronghold of my life—
of whom shall I be afraid?
When the wicked advance against me
to devour me,
it is my enemies and my foes
who will stumble and fall.
Though an army besiege me,
my heart will not fear;
though war break out against me,
even then I will be confident.
One thing I ask from the Lord,
this only do I seek:
that I may dwell in the house of the Lord
all the days of my life,
to gaze on the beauty of the Lord
and to seek him in his temple.
For in the day of trouble
he will keep me safe in his dwelling;
he will hide me in the shelter of his sacred tent
and set me high upon a rock.
Then my head will be exalted
above the enemies who surround me;
at his sacred tent I will sacrifice with shouts of joy;
I will sing and make music to the Lord.

continued . . .

Hear my voice when I call, Lord;
be merciful to me and answer me.
My heart says of you, "Seek his face!"
Your face, Lord, I will seek.
Do not hide your face from me,
do not turn your servant away in anger;
you have been my helper.
Do not reject me or forsake me,
God my Savior.
Though my father and mother forsake me,
the Lord will receive me.

I'll Take Him

Though my father and my mother forsake me,
the LORD will receive me.
—PSALM 27:10

Years ago, when I was a student at the University of California at Berkeley, I developed a friendship with a fellow student who had suffered a terrible loss. His child had died, and his wife had left him because she couldn't deal with the pain.

One day, as my friend and I were walking down the street, we found ourselves behind a disheveled mother with a grubby little boy in hand. She was angry at the child and was walking much too fast, towing him at a pace his little legs couldn't maintain.

We reached a busy intersection where the child abruptly stopped and his hand slipped out of his mother's grasp. She turned around, spat out a curse, and trudged on. The little boy sat down on the curb and burst into tears. Without a moment's hesitation, my friend sat down next to him and gathered the little guy in his arms.

The woman turned and, looking at the child, began to curse again. My friend sighed and looked up. "Lady," he said softly, "If you don't want him, I'll take him."

So it is with our Father in heaven. He too has known great loss and loves us just as tenderly. Even if our friends and family forsake us, our God never will (Psalm 27:10). We are ever in His care.

If God cares for sparrows,
He surely cares for us.

The righteous will flourish like a palm tree,
they will grow like a cedar of Lebanon;
planted in the house of the LORD,
they will flourish in the courts of our God.
They will still bear fruit in old age,
they will stay fresh and green,
proclaiming, "The LORD is upright;
he is my Rock, and there is no wickedness in him."

The Red Hackle

They will still bear fruit in old age,
they will stay fresh and green.
—PSALM 92:14

Several years ago, I stumbled across a bit of fishing lore in a second-century AD work by the Greek writer Aelian. In *On the Nature of Animals*, he wrote, "Between Boroca and Thessalonica runs a river called the Astracus, and in it there are fish with spotted skins [trout]." He then describes a "snare for the fish, by which they get the better of them. They fastened crimson red wool round a hook and attached two feathers. Then they would throw their snare, and the fish, attracted by the color, comes up, thinking to get a mouthful."

Fishermen still use this lure today. It is called the Red Hackle. First used over 2,200 years ago, it remains a snare for trout by which we "get the better of them."

When I read that ancient work I thought: Not all old things are passé—especially people. If through contented and cheerful old age we show others the fullness and deepness of God, we'll be useful to the end of our days. Old age does not have to focus on declining health, pining over what once was. It can also be full of tranquility and mirth and courage and kindness, the fruit of those who have grown old with God.

"Those who are planted in the house of the LORD . . . shall still bear fruit in old age; they shall be fresh and flourishing" (Psalm 92:13–14 NKJV).

Lord, thank you for your faithfulness throughout our lives. Help us finish our lives well in service to you and to remember that old age does not mean uselessness.

As the years add up,
God's faithfulness keeps multiplying.

Where can I go from your Spirit?
Where can I flee from your presence?
If I go up to the heavens, you are there;
if I make my bed in the depths, you are there.
If I rise on the wings of the dawn,
if I settle on the far side of the sea,
even there your hand will guide me,
your right hand will hold me fast.
If I say, "Surely the darkness will hide me
and the light become night around me,"
even the darkness will not be dark to you;
the night will shine like the day,
for darkness is as light to you.

One Who Understands

For we do not have a high priest
who is unable to empathize with our weaknesses,
but we have one who has been tempted in every way,
just as we are—yet he did not sin.
—HEBREWS 4:15

My friend's husband was in the last stages of dementia. In his first introduction to the nurse who was assigned to care for him, he reached out for her arm and stopped her. He said he wanted to introduce her to his best friend—one who loved him deeply.

Since no one else was in the hall, the nurse thought he was delusional. But as it turned out, he was speaking of Jesus. She was deeply touched but had to hurry on to care for another patient. When she returned, the darkness had closed in again and the man was no longer lucid.

Even though this man had descended into the darkness of dementia, he knew that the Lord was his best Friend. God dwells in the fathomless depth that is our soul. He can pierce the darkest mind and assure us of His tender, loving care. Indeed, the darkness shall not hide us from Him (Psalm 139:12).

We do not know what the future holds for us or those we love. We too may descend into the darkness of mental illness, Alzheimer's, or dementia as we age. But even there the Lord's hand will lead us, and His right hand will hold us tight (v. 10). We cannot get away from His love and personal care.

Jesus loves me.
This I know.

Our days may come to seventy years,
or eighty, if our strength endures;
yet the best of them are but trouble and sorrow,
for they quickly pass, and we fly away.
If only we knew the power of your anger!
Your wrath is as great as the fear that is your due.
Teach us to number our days,
that we may gain a heart of wisdom.
Relent, LORD! How long will it be?
Have compassion on your servants.
Satisfy us in the morning with your unfailing love,
that we may sing for joy and be glad all our days.
Make us glad for as many days as you have afflicted us,
for as many years as we have seen trouble.
May your deeds be shown to your servants,
your splendor to their children.
May the favor of the Lord our God rest on us;
establish the work of our hands for us—
yes, establish the work of our hands.

Time Flies

Teach us to number our days,
that we may gain a heart of wisdom.
—PSALM 90:12

Many metaphors are used in literature to describe life's brevity. It is a dream, a swift runner, a mist, a puff of smoke, a shadow, a gesture in the air, a sentence written in the sand, a bird flying in one window of a house and out another. Another symbolic description was suggested by a friend of mine who said that the short dash between the dates of birth and death on tombstones represents the brief span of one's life.

When we were children, time loitered. But as we get closer to the end of our lives, time moves with increasing swiftness, like water swirling down a drain. In childhood we measured our age in small increments. "I'm six and a half," we would say, for it seemed to take so long to get older. Now we have no time for such childishness. Who claims to be sixty and a half?

It's good to ponder the brevity of life now and then. Life is too short to treat it carelessly. In Psalm 90, after describing the shortness of life, Moses prayed, "Teach us to number our days, that we may gain a heart of wisdom" (v. 12).

To make the most of our earthly existence, we must lose ourselves in the will of God (1 Peter 4:2). This we can do even when time is running out. It's never too late to give ourselves totally to God.

Don't just count your days,
make your days count.

When my heart was grieved
and my spirit embittered,
I was senseless and ignorant;
I was a brute beast before you.
Yet I am always with you;
you hold me by my right hand.
You guide me with your counsel,
and afterward you will take me into glory.
Whom have I in heaven but you?
And earth has nothing I desire besides you.
My flesh and my heart may fail,
but God is the strength of my heart
and my portion forever.
Those who are far from you will perish;
you destroy all who are unfaithful to you.
But as for me, it is good to be near God.
I have made the Sovereign Lord my refuge;
I will tell of all your deeds.

The Good Life

It is good to be near God.
—PSALM 73:28

Beauty, wealth, power, love, marriage, and pleasure are good things, but they're not the best. The best is loving God and taking in His love—bringing Him glory and making Him our friend for life. That leads to the best possible life because it gives us satisfaction and joy now (John 10:10), and it's what Christians are going to be doing forever.

That's why we should make time for God and rest in His love—the love that made you and me. It is the reason for our existence and the means by which we will make the most of our lives.

I like the way the psalmist put it: "It is good to be near God. I have made the Sovereign LORD my refuge; I will tell of all your deeds" (Psalm 73:28). In other words, the good life is drawing close to the One who loves us like no other.

And how can we "be near" Him? Here's a practice I began many years ago: Take a few minutes every morning to read some verses from the Gospels (Matthew, Mark, Luke, John) and note what Jesus said or did. After all, He came to show us what God is like (Hebrews 1:1–3). Put yourself in the story—in the place of the leper He healed with His loving touch, for example (Mark 1:40–45). Think about how much He loves you, and then thank Him!

> **The wonder of it all—
> just to think that Jesus loves me!**

Answer me when I call to you,
my righteous God.
Give me relief from my distress;
have mercy on me and hear my prayer.
How long will you people turn my glory into shame?
How long will you love delusions and seek false gods?
Know that the LORD has set apart
his faithful servant for himself;
the LORD hears when I call to him.
Tremble and do not sin;
when you are on your beds,
search your hearts and be silent.
Offer the sacrifices of the righteous
and trust in the LORD.
Many, LORD, are asking, "Who will bring us prosperity?"
Let the light of your face shine on us.
Fill my heart with joy
when their grain and new wine abound.
In peace I will lie down and sleep,
for you alone, LORD,
make me dwell in safety.

Forever Loved

Know that the LORD has set apart
his faithful servant for himself.
—PSALM 4:3

It's almost impossible for us to get through a day without being snubbed, ignored, or put down in some way. Sometimes we even do it to ourselves.

David's enemies were talking smack—bullying, threatening, pummeling him with insults. His sense of self-worth and well-being had plummeted (Psalm 4:1–2). He asked for relief "from my distress."

Then David remembered, "Know that the LORD has set apart his faithful servant for himself" (v. 3). Various English versions try to capture the full essence of David's bold statement by translating "faithful servant" as "godly." The Hebrew word here, *hesed*, literally refers to God's covenant love and might well be rendered "those whom God will love forever and ever and ever."

Here's what we too must remember: We are loved forever, set apart in a special way, as dear to God as His own Son. He has called us to be His children for all eternity.

Instead of despairing, we can remind ourselves of the love we freely receive from our Father. We are His dearly beloved children. The end is not despair but peace and joy (vv. 7–8). He never gives up on us, and He never ever stops loving us.

The true measure of God's love
is that He loves without measure.
—BERNARD OF CLAIRVAUX

Hear us, Shepherd of Israel,
you who lead Joseph like a flock.
You who sit enthroned between the cherubim,
shine forth before Ephraim, Benjamin and Manasseh.
Awaken your might;
come and save us.
Restore us, O God;
make your face shine on us,
that we may be saved.
How long, LORD God Almighty,
will your anger smolder
against the prayers of your people?
You have fed them with the bread of tears;
you have made them drink tears by the bowlful.
You have made us an object of derision to our neighbors,
and our enemies mock us.
Restore us, God Almighty;
make your face shine on us,
that we may be saved.
You transplanted a vine from Egypt;
you drove out the nations and planted it.
You cleared the ground for it,
and it took root and filled the land.

The mountains were covered with its shade,
the mighty cedars with its branches.
Its branches reached as far as the Sea,
its shoots as far as the River.
Why have you broken down its walls
so that all who pass by pick its grapes?
Boars from the forest ravage it,
and insects from the fields feed on it.
Return to us, God Almighty!
Look down from heaven and see!
Watch over this vine,
the root your right hand has planted,
the son you have raised up for yourself.
Your vine is cut down, it is burned with fire;
at your rebuke your people perish.
Let your hand rest on the man at your right hand,
the son of man you have raised up for yourself.
Then we will not turn away from you;
revive us, and we will call on your name.
Restore us, Lord God Almighty;
make your face shine on us,
that we may be saved.

Our Father's Face

Restore us, O God;
make your face shine on us,
that we may be saved.
—PSALM 80:3

I remember my father's face. It was hard to read. He was a kind man, but stoic and self-contained. As a child, I often searched his face, looking for a smile or other show of affection. Faces are us. A frown, a sullen look, a smile, and crinkly eyes reveal what we feel about others. Our faces are our "tell."

Asaph, the author of Psalm 80, was distraught and wanted to see the Lord's face. He looked north from his vantage point in Jerusalem and saw Judah's sister-state, Israel, collapse under the weight of the Assyrian Empire. With her buffer state gone, Judah was vulnerable to invasion from all sides—Assyria from the north, Egypt from the south, and the Arab nations from the east. She was outnumbered and outmatched.

Asaph gathered up his fears in a prayer, three times repeated (80:3, 7, 19), "Make your face shine on us, that we may be saved." (Or, in other words, "let me see Your smile.")

It's good to look away from our fears and search our heavenly Father's face. The best way to see God's face is to look at the cross. The cross is His "tell" (John 3:16).

So know this: When your Father looks at you, He has a great big smile on His face. You're very safe!

God's love for us is as expansive as the open arms of Christ on the cross.

The LORD makes firm the steps
of the one who delights in him;
though he may stumble, he will not fall,
for the LORD upholds him with his hand.
I was young and now I am old,
yet I have never seen the righteous forsaken
or their children begging bread.
They are always generous and lend freely;
their children will be a blessing.
Turn from evil and do good;
then you will dwell in the land forever.
For the LORD loves the just
and will not forsake his faithful ones.
Wrongdoers will be completely destroyed;
the offspring of the wicked will perish.
The righteous will inherit the land
and dwell in it forever.
The mouths of the righteous utter wisdom,
and their tongues speak what is just.
The law of their God is in their hearts;
their feet do not slip.
The wicked lie in wait for the righteous,
intent on putting them to death;
but the LORD will not leave them in the power of the wicked
or let them be condemned when brought to trial.

continued . . .

Hope in the LORD
and keep his way.
He will exalt you to inherit the land;
when the wicked are destroyed, you will see it.
I have seen a wicked and ruthless man
flourishing like a luxuriant native tree,
but he soon passed away and was no more;
though I looked for him, he could not be found.
Consider the blameless, observe the upright;
a future awaits those who seek peace.
But all sinners will be destroyed;
there will be no future for the wicked.
The salvation of the righteous comes from the LORD;
he is their stronghold in time of trouble.
The LORD helps them and delivers them;
he delivers them from the wicked and saves them,
because they take refuge in him.

God's Will

The LORD makes firm the steps
of the one who delights in him.
—PSALM 37:23

We're often looking for God's will—especially when we're in a difficult situation. We wonder, *What will happen to me here? Should I stay or does God want me somewhere else?* The only way to know for sure is to do what He asks you to do right now—the duty of the present moment—and wait for God to reveal the next step.

As you obey what you know, you will be strengthened to take the next step and the next. Step by step, one step at a time. That's how we learn to walk with God.

But you say, "Suppose I take the first step. What will happen next?" That's God's business. Your task and mine is to obey this day and leave the future to Him. The psalmist says "the LORD makes firm the steps of the one who delights in him" (37:23). This day's direction is all we need. Tomorrow's instruction is of no use to us at all. George MacDonald said, "We do not understand the next page of God's lesson book; we see only the one before us. Nor shall we be allowed to turn the leaf until we have learned its lesson."

If we concern ourselves with God's will and obey each day the directions and warnings He gives, if we walk by faith and step out in the path of obedience, we will find that God will lead us through this day. As Jesus put it, "Tomorrow will worry about itself" (Matthew 6:34).

Blessed is the person who finds out
which way God is moving
and then goes in that direction.

The Lord says to my lord:
"Sit at my right hand
until I make your enemies
a footstool for your feet."
The Lord will extend your mighty scepter from Zion, saying,
"Rule in the midst of your enemies!"
Your troops will be willing
on your day of battle.
Arrayed in holy splendor,
your young men will come to you
like dew from the morning's womb.
The Lord has sworn
and will not change his mind:
"You are a priest forever,
in the order of Melchizedek."
The Lord is at your right hand;
he will crush kings on the day of his wrath.
He will judge the nations, heaping up the dead
and crushing the rulers of the whole earth.
He will drink from a brook along the way,
and so he will lift his head high.

A Difficult Hill

He will drink from a brook along the way,
and so he will lift his head high.
—PSALM 110:7

High in a fold of Jughandle Peak in the mountains north of our home in Idaho lies a glacial lake. The route to the lake goes up a steep, exposed ridge through boulders and loose stones. It's a strenuous ascent.

At the beginning of the climb, however, there is a brook—a spring that seeps out of soft, mossy earth and flows through a lush meadow. It's a quiet place to drink deeply and prepare for the hard climb ahead.

In John Bunyan's classic allegory of the Christian life, *The Pilgrim's Progress*, Christian arrives at the foot of a steep ascent called the Hill Difficulty, "at the bottom of which was a spring . . . Christian now went to the spring and drank to refresh himself, and then began to go up the hill."

Perhaps the difficult mountain you face is a rebellious child or a serious medical diagnosis. The challenge seems more than you can endure.

Before you face your next major task, visit the spring of refreshment that is God himself. Come to Him with all your weakness, weariness, helplessness, fear, and doubt. Then drink deeply of His power, strength, and wisdom. God knows all your circumstances and will supply a store of comfort, of spiritual strengthening and consolation. He will lift up your head and give you strength to go on.

> He who overrules all things . . .
> enabled Christian to . . . continue on his way.
> —JOHN BUNYAN, *THE PILGRIM'S PROGRESS*

How long, Lord? Will you forget me forever?
How long will you hide your face from me?
How long must I wrestle with my thoughts
and day after day have sorrow in my heart?
How long will my enemy triumph over me?
Look on me and answer, Lord my God.
Give light to my eyes, or I will sleep in death,
and my enemy will say, "I have overcome him,"
and my foes will rejoice when I fall.
But I trust in your unfailing love;
my heart rejoices in your salvation.
I will sing the Lord's praise,
for he has been good to me.

How Long?

How long, LORD?
Will you forget me forever?
—PSALM 13:1

For nine long years, Saul hounded David as "one hunts a partridge in the mountains" (1 Samuel 26:20). "How long, LORD? Will you forget me forever?" David prayed. "How long will you hide your face from me? . . . How long will my enemy triumph over me?" (Psalm 13:1–2).

Prolonged affliction often vexes us as well. We want a sudden solution, a quick fix. But some things can't be fixed. They can only be borne.

But we can complain to God in our troubles. We have a heavenly Father who wants us to engage with Him in our struggles. He understands His children as no one else can.

When we turn to Him with our complaints, we come to our senses. In David's case, his thoughts went back to life's certainty: God's love. David reminded himself: "I trust in your unfailing love; my heart rejoices in your salvation. I will sing the LORD's praise, for he has been good to me" (vv. 5–6). Sufferings may persist, but David could sing in the midst of his trials, for he was God's beloved child. That's all he needed to know.

A. W. Thorold writes, "The highest pinnacle of the spiritual life is not happy joy in unbroken sunshine, but absolute and undoubting trust in the love of God."

Even in our troubles, God's love can be trusted.

God's love stands
when all else fails.

For he will deliver the needy who cry out,
the afflicted who have no one to help.
He will take pity on the weak and the needy
and save the needy from death.
He will rescue them from oppression and violence,
for precious is their blood in his sight.
Long may he live!
May gold from Sheba be given him.
May people ever pray for him
and bless him all day long.
May grain abound throughout the land;
on the tops of the hills may it sway.
May the crops flourish like Lebanon
and thrive like the grass of the field.
May his name endure forever;
may it continue as long as the sun.
Then all nations will be blessed through him,
and they will call him blessed.
Praise be to the LORD God, the God of Israel,
who alone does marvelous deeds.
Praise be to his glorious name forever;
may the whole earth be filled with his glory.
Amen and Amen.
This concludes the prayers of David son of Jesse.

Grain on the Mountaintop

There will be an abundance of grain in the earth,
on the top of the mountains.
—PSALM 72:16 (NKJV)

I've been on a number of mountaintops in the US in my time, and I can tell you that not much grows up there. The summits of mountains are bare rock and lichen. That's not where you would normally find an abundance of grain.

But Solomon, who wrote Psalm 72, asked God for "an abundance of grain . . . on the top of the mountains," to characterize his reign as king (NKJV). If grain on the mountain is so unusual, what is Solomon suggesting? That God's power can produce results in even the most unpromising soil?

Perhaps you think of yourself as a little person, with very little to bring to the kingdom. Take courage: God can produce an abundant harvest through you. This is one of the ironies of faith: God uses the insignificant to accomplish the great. Not many of us are wise or noble; most of us are anonymous and far from extraordinary. Yet all of us can be used. And contrary to what we might think, it is because of our weakness that we can be used by God (1 Corinthians 1:27–29; 2 Corinthians 12:10).

It's possible to be too big or proud for God to use, but we can never be too little. "Out of weakness" we are "made strong" (Hebrews 11:34 NKJV). By God's great power, we can do all that He has called us to do.

> To experience God's power,
> we must first admit that we are weak.

The trees of the Lord are well watered,
the cedars of Lebanon that he planted.
There the birds make their nests;
the stork has its home in the junipers.
The high mountains belong to the wild goats;
the crags are a refuge for the hyrax.
He made the moon to mark the seasons,
and the sun knows when to go down.
You bring darkness, it becomes night,
and all the beasts of the forest prowl.
The lions roar for their prey
and seek their food from God.
The sun rises, and they steal away;
they return and lie down in their dens.
Then people go out to their work,
to their labor until evening.
How many are your works, Lord!
In wisdom you made them all;
the earth is full of your creatures.
There is the sea, vast and spacious,
teeming with creatures beyond number—
living things both large and small.

The Trail

He has made everything beautiful in its time.
He has also set eternity in the human heart;
yet no one can fathom what God has done
from beginning to end.
—ECCLESIASTES 3:11

High in the mountains near our home is a trail that threads its way, rising and falling down the side of a steep canyon. It leads to a stream that passes first through a castle-like heap of boulders, then flows gently through deep, mossy woods. It's a peaceful, quiet area where wild flowers bloom in fragile beauty—a secluded, seldom-visited place.

Even if no one ever saw this place, it would still be beautiful, because God creates beauty for its own sake. But the marvelous thing is that He created this beauty for anyone who will receive it, as a visible expression of His creativity and His love. This is my reason to look into nature, my reason to explore.

I worship and thank God for this restful hideaway. With David, I exclaim, "How many are your works, Lord! In wisdom you made them all; the earth is full of your creatures" (Psalm 104:24).

I feel sorry for those who worship nature itself and who do not know God, its Creator. When they come to places like this, they have no one to thank.

We who know God recognize Him in creation, and we can always thank Him for showing His love in such beautiful ways.

**Creation is filled with signs
that point to the Creator.**

Praise awaits you, our God, in Zion;
to you our vows will be fulfilled.
You who answer prayer,
to you all people will come.
When we were overwhelmed by sins,
you forgave our transgressions.
Blessed are those you choose
and bring near to live in your courts!
We are filled with the good things of your house,
of your holy temple.
You answer us with awesome and righteous deeds,
God our Savior,
the hope of all the ends of the earth
and of the farthest seas,
who formed the mountains by your power,
having armed yourself with strength,
who stilled the roaring of the seas,
the roaring of their waves,
and the turmoil of the nations.
The whole earth is filled with awe at your wonders;
where morning dawns, where evening fades,
you call forth songs of joy.
You care for the land and water it;
you enrich it abundantly.
The streams of God are filled with water
to provide the people with grain,
for so you have ordained it.
You drench its furrows and level its ridges;
you soften it with showers and bless its crops.
You crown the year with your bounty,
and your carts overflow with abundance.
The grasslands of the wilderness overflow;
the hills are clothed with gladness.
The meadows are covered with flocks
and the valleys are mantled with grain;
they shout for joy and sing.

Squirrel Feeder

You crown the year with your bounty,
and your carts overflow with abundance.
—PSALM 65:11

Some years ago, I placed a squirrel feeder on a fir tree a few yards from our home. It's a simple device—two boards and a nail on which to impale a corncob. Each morning a squirrel comes to enjoy that day's meal. She's a pretty thing—black with a round, gray tummy.

I sit on our back porch in the morning and watch her eat. She plucks each kernel from the cob, holds it in her paws, turns it around and eats the heart out of the kernel. At the end of the day no kernels remain, only a neat little pile of leftovers under the tree.

Despite my care for her, the creature is afraid of me. When I approach, she runs away, taking refuge in her tree and chattering at me when I get too close. She doesn't know that I provide for her.

Some people are like that with God. They run from Him in fear. They don't know that He loves them and richly provides them with everything for their enjoyment (Psalm 65:11).

Henry Scougal, a seventeenth-century Scottish minister, wrote, "Nothing is more powerful to engage our affection than to find that we are [loved by] One who is altogether lovely. . . . How must this astonish and delight us; how must it overcome our [fear] and melt our hearts." God's love is the perfect love that "drives out fear" (1 John 4:18).

**Your loving heavenly Father
never takes His eyes off you.**

Blessed are those whose strength is in you,
whose hearts are set on pilgrimage.
As they pass through the Valley of Baka,
they make it a place of springs;
the autumn rains also cover it with pools.
They go from strength to strength,
till each appears before God in Zion.
Hear my prayer, Lord God Almighty;
listen to me, God of Jacob.
Look on our shield, O God;
look with favor on your anointed one.
Better is one day in your courts
than a thousand elsewhere;
I would rather be a doorkeeper in the house of my God
than dwell in the tents of the wicked.
For the Lord God is a sun and shield;
the Lord bestows favor and honor;
no good thing does he withhold
from those whose walk is blameless.
Lord Almighty,
blessed is the one who trusts in you.

Grace and Glory

The LORD will give grace and glory;
No good thing will He withhold
from those who walk uprightly.
—PSALM 84:11 (NKJV)

There's a circular path in the park where I walk behind our home in Boise, Idaho. When I've walked three times around, I've gone one mile.

It's easy to lose count of the laps on my three-mile walk. So each morning I pick up nine small stones and put them in my pocket, discarding one each time I finish a lap.

I always feel good when there's one stone left in my pocket. It puts spring in my step. I pick up the pace.

It occurs to me that my walk through life is a lot like those daily walks. I've completed three-score and ten years and don't have far to go. That too puts spring in my step.

I'm in no hurry to leave this life, but my times are in God's hands. As the body is breaking down under the weight of the years, there is a grace within that sustains me. I go now "from strength to strength," and in good time I will appear "before God in Zion" (Psalm 84:7). That will be glory for me.

Our Lord gives "grace and glory," the psalmist says—grace for our earthly walk and glory when we have finished it. "No good thing will He withhold from those who walk uprightly" (v. 11 NKJV).

Do you need grace today? God gives it with both hands. All you have to do is take it.

God gives grace for this life and glory in the life to come.

As the deer pants for streams of water,
so my soul pants for you, my God.
My soul thirsts for God, for the living God.
When can I go and meet with God?
My tears have been my food
day and night,
while people say to me all day long,
"Where is your God?"
These things I remember
as I pour out my soul:
how I used to go to the house of God
under the protection of the Mighty One
with shouts of joy and praise
among the festive throng.
Why, my soul, are you downcast?
Why so disturbed within me?
Put your hope in God,
for I will yet praise him,
my Savior and my God.
My soul is downcast within me;
therefore I will remember you
from the land of the Jordan,
the heights of Hermon—from Mount Mizar.

Deep calls to deep
in the roar of your waterfalls;
all your waves and breakers
have swept over me.
By day the LORD directs his love,
at night his song is with me—
a prayer to the God of my life.
I say to God my Rock,
"Why have you forgotten me?
Why must I go about mourning,
oppressed by the enemy?"
My bones suffer mortal agony
as my foes taunt me,
saying to me all day long,
"Where is your God?"
Why, my soul, are you downcast?
Why so disturbed within me?
Put your hope in God,
for I will yet praise him,
my Savior and my God.

Johnny's Cap

As for me, I will always have hope;
I will praise you more and more.
—PSALM 71:14

A story is told about a family that went on a picnic by a lake. At one point, their five-year-old son waded into the lake, stepped into deep water, and sank out of sight. None of the adults in the family knew how to swim, so they ran up and down the shore in panic while the child bobbed up and down and screamed for help. Just then, a man happened by who sized up the situation, leaped into the lake, and rescued the boy. He climbed out on the bank with the child, who was frightened but unharmed, only to hear the mother ask with irritation, "Where's Johnny's cap?"

So often we focus on small disappointments that cause us to grumble and complain rather than focusing on the wonderful things God has brought into our lives, not the least of which is His everlasting love and eternal salvation. When we complain about the small dissatisfactions of life, we're asking, in effect, "Where's Johnny's cap?"

Paul wrote, "In everything give thanks" (1 Thessalonians 5:18 NKJV). We may not be thankful for everything that comes our way, but we can give thanks in everything. It may be difficult to be grateful when we lose our job or our health fails, but we can be thankful for the good that God has brought to us in this life and grateful for the life to come.

Instead of being preoccupied with our problems,
let's praise the Lord for His blessings.

In you, LORD, I have taken refuge;
let me never be put to shame;
deliver me in your righteousness.
Turn your ear to me,
come quickly to my rescue;
be my rock of refuge,
a strong fortress to save me.
Since you are my rock and my fortress,
for the sake of your name lead and guide me.
Keep me free from the trap that is set for me,
for you are my refuge.
Into your hands I commit my spirit;
deliver me, Lord, my faithful God.
I hate those who cling to worthless idols;
as for me, I trust in the LORD.
I will be glad and rejoice in your love,
for you saw my affliction
and knew the anguish of my soul.
You have not given me into the hands of the enemy
but have set my feet in a spacious place.
Be merciful to me, LORD, for I am in distress;
my eyes grow weak with sorrow,
my soul and body with grief.

continued . . .

My life is consumed by anguish
and my years by groaning;
my strength fails because of my affliction,
and my bones grow weak.
Because of all my enemies,
I am the utter contempt of my neighbors
and an object of dread to my closest friends—
those who see me on the street flee from me.
I am forgotten as though I were dead;
I have become like broken pottery.
For I hear many whispering,
"Terror on every side!"
They conspire against me
and plot to take my life.
But I trust in you, LORD;
I say, "You are my God."

God's Tender Care

You saw my affliction and
knew the anguish of my soul.
—PSALM 31:7

During a time of grief, C. S. Lewis observed that his neighbors walked across the street to avoid him when they saw him approaching.

David too knew a time of grief when he said, "I am a reproach among all my enemies, but especially among my neighbors. . . . I am forgotten like a dead man" (Psalm 31:11–12 NKJV).

Perhaps you've known times when friends seem to forget you in your sorrow. They fail to call, or write, or promise to pray.

But those are the times when we can sense God's tenderness most deeply. When the days are long and lonely and no one seems to care, He seeks us out and surrounds us with lovingkindness. Our sorrow, far from burdening Him, draws out His tender compassion. He knows the troubles of our soul (v. 7). And He cares. Thus we can commit our spirit into His hand (v. 5), as our Lord Jesus did when all forsook Him and fled.

Songwriter Frank Graeff asks, "Does Jesus care when my heart is pained too deeply for mirth and song; as the burdens press, and the cares distress, and the way grows weary and long?" The answer? Yes! He invites us to give our burdens and cares to Him, because He cares for us (1 Peter 5:7).

Trust God to care for you today.

**We can never get beyond
the circle of God's care.**

Your righteousness, God, reaches to the heavens,
you who have done great things.
Who is like you, God?
Though you have made me see troubles,
many and bitter,
you will restore my life again;
from the depths of the earth
you will again bring me up.
You will increase my honor
and comfort me once more.
I will praise you with the harp
for your faithfulness, my God;
I will sing praise to you with the lyre,
Holy One of Israel.
My lips will shout for joy
when I sing praise to you—
I whom you have delivered.
My tongue will tell of your righteous acts
all day long,
for those who wanted to harm me
have been put to shame and confusion.

Perfect Peace and Rest

Though you have made me see troubles,
many and bitter, you will restore my life again.
—PSALM 71:20

The psalmist had seen "troubles, many and bitter" (Psalm 71:20). Yet hovering in the back of his mind was the thought that God would "revive" him again. The literal meaning of this phrase is "bring him to life again." He elaborated: "You will restore my life again; from the depths of the earth you will again bring me up. You will increase my honor and comfort me once more" (vv. 20–21). If the troubles didn't end in this life, certainly in heaven they would.

This thought—that someday we shall be in God's presence and enjoy Him forever—crowns many of the Psalms and is an assurance that helps life's present troubles fade away (see Psalm 16, 17, 49, 73).

Perhaps no one but God knows the trouble you've seen, but this is not all that shall be. Someday, your Father will "increase [your] honor"—you will be clothed with unspeakable glory. There will be comfort "once more." His presence and love will bring perfect peace and rest.

Richard Baxter writes, "O, what a blessed day that will be when I shall . . . stand on the shore and look back on the raging seas I have safely passed; when I shall review my pains and sorrows, my fears and tears, and possess the glory which was the end of all!"

When God wipes our tears,
sorrow will give way to eternal song.

Lord, who may dwell in your sacred tent?
Who may live on your holy mountain?
The one whose walk is blameless,
who does what is righteous,
who speaks the truth from their heart;
whose tongue utters no slander,
who does no wrong to a neighbor,
and casts no slur on others;
who despises a vile person
but honors those who fear the Lord;
who keeps an oath even when it hurts,
and does not change their mind;
who lends money to the poor without interest;
who does not accept a bribe against the innocent.
Whoever does these things
will never be shaken.

An Honest Heart

I know, my God,
that you test the heart and
are pleased with integrity.
—1 CHRONICLES 29:17

I came across an epitaph on an old gravestone in a cemetery the other day. It read, "J. Holgate: An honest man."

I know nothing of Holgate's life, but because his marker is unusually ornate, he must have struck it rich. But whatever he accomplished in his lifetime, he's remembered for just one thing: He was "an honest man."

Diogenes, the Greek philosopher, spent a lifetime in search of honesty and finally concluded that an honest man could not be found. Honest people are hard to find in any age, but the trait is one that greatly matters. Honesty is not the best policy; it's the only policy, and one of the marks of a man or woman who lives in God's presence. David writes, "LORD, . . . who may live on your holy mountain? The one whose walk is blameless" (Psalm 15:1–2).

I ask myself: Am I trustworthy and honorable in all my affairs? Do my words ring true? Do I speak the truth in love or do I fudge and fade the facts now and then, or exaggerate for emphasis? If so, I may turn to God with complete confidence and ask for forgiveness and for a good and honest heart—to make truthfulness an integral part of my nature. The One who has begun a good work in me is faithful. He will do it.

> Live in such a way that when
> people think of honesty and integrity,
> they will think of you.

Sing joyfully to the Lord, you righteous;
it is fitting for the upright to praise him.
Praise the Lord with the harp;
make music to him on the ten-stringed lyre.
Sing to him a new song;
play skillfully, and shout for joy.
For the word of the Lord is right and true;
he is faithful in all he does.
The Lord loves righteousness and justice;
the earth is full of his unfailing love.

A New Song

Praise the LORD with the harp;
make music to him on the ten-stringed lyre.
Sing to him a new song.
—PSALM 33:2–3

I was walking in the park one morning, listening to a tape by the Brooklyn Tabernacle Choir. I had my ancient Walkman clipped to my belt and my headphones clamped over my ears, tuned in to another world. The music was joyous! Oblivious to my surroundings, I began to sing and dance.

Then I spied my neighbor, leaning against a tree with a bemused look on her face. She couldn't hear my music, but she was delighted by my behavior. I wish she could have heard my song.

I thought afterward of the new song God has placed in our hearts, a song we hear from another world. It tells us that God loves us and always will, and that He has "rescued us from the dominion of darkness" (Colossians 1:13) and "seated us with him in the heavenly realms in Christ Jesus" (Ephesians 2:6). And someday He'll take us to be with Him forever.

In the meantime He has given us eternally useful things to do. Grace now and glory ahead! Is this not a reason to sing?

Next time you're down in the dumps, think about God's goodness. Tune in to the music of heaven and sing a new song with the angels. It may set your feet to dancing and cause great wonderment in those around you. Perhaps they'll want to hear the music too.

God's work in our life
puts a new song in our heart.

I call to you, LORD, come quickly to me;
hear me when I call to you.
May my prayer be set before you like incense;
may the lifting up of my hands be like the evening sacrifice.
Set a guard over my mouth, LORD;
keep watch over the door of my lips.

Constant Kindness

Be kind and compassionate
to one another.
—EPHESIANS 4:32

When I was a child I was an ardent reader of L. Frank Baum's Land of Oz books. I recently came across *Rinkitink in Oz* with all the original artwork. I laughed again at the antics of Baum's irrepressible, good-hearted King Rinkitink with his down-to-earth goodness. Young Prince Inga described him best: "His heart is kind and gentle and that is far better than being wise."

How simple and how sensible! Yet who among us has not wounded the heart of someone dear to us by a harsh word? By doing so, we disturb the peace and quiet of the hour and we can undo much of the good we have done toward those we love. "A small unkindness is a great offense," said Hannah More, an eighteenth-century English writer.

Here's the good news: Anyone can become kind. We may be incapable of preaching an inspiring sermon, fielding hard questions, or evangelizing vast numbers, but we can all be kind.

How? Through prayer. It is the only way to soften our hearts. "Set a guard over my mouth, LORD; keep watch over the door of my lips. Do not let my heart be drawn to what is evil" (Psalm 141:3–4).

In a world in which love has grown cold, a kindness that comes from the heart of God is one of the most helpful and healing things we can offer to others.

The knowledge that God has loved me
beyond all limits will compel me to go into
the world to love others in the same way.
—OSWALD CHAMBERS

Give thanks to the LORD, for he is good;
his love endures forever.
Let the redeemed of the LORD tell their story—
those he redeemed from the hand of the foe,
those he gathered from the lands,
from east and west, from north and south.
Some wandered in desert wastelands,
finding no way to a city where they could settle.
They were hungry and thirsty,
and their lives ebbed away.
Then they cried out to the LORD in their trouble,
and he delivered them from their distress.
He led them by a straight way
to a city where they could settle.
Let them give thanks to the LORD for his unfailing love
and his wonderful deeds for mankind,
for he satisfies the thirsty
and fills the hungry with good things.

Not All Empty

He satisfies the thirsty
and fills the hungry
with good things.
—PSALM 107:9

Our granddaughter Julia spent the summer working in an orphanage in Busia, Uganda. On the final day of her internship, she went to the children to tell each one goodbye. One little girl named Sumaya was very sad and said to her, "Tomorrow you leave us, and next week the other aunties [interns] leave."

When Julia agreed that she was indeed leaving, Sumaya thought for a minute and exclaimed, "But we will be all empty. None of you will be left!" Again, Julia agreed. The little girl thought a few moments and replied: "But God will be with us, so we won't be all empty."

If we are honest with ourselves, we know that "all empty" feeling. It is an emptiness that friendship, love, sex, money, power, popularity, or success can never assuage—a longing for something indefinable, something incalculably precious but lost. Every good thing can remind, beckon, and awaken in us a greater desire for that elusive "something more." The closest we get is a hint, an echo in a face, a painting, a scene. . . . And then it is gone. "Our best havings are wantings," said C. S. Lewis.

We were made for God, and in the end, nothing less will satisfy us. Without Him, we are all empty. He alone fills the hungry with good things (Psalm 107:9).

God cannot give us a happiness and peace apart from Himself because it is not there.
—C. S. LEWIS

Praise the LORD.
How good it is to sing praises to our God,
how pleasant and fitting to praise him!
The LORD builds up Jerusalem;
he gathers the exiles of Israel.
He heals the brokenhearted
and binds up their wounds.
He determines the number of the stars
and calls them each by name.
Great is our Lord and mighty in power;
his understanding has no limit.

A Tender and Mighty God

[God] heals the brokenhearted
and binds up their wounds.
He determines the number of the stars
and calls them each by name.
—PSALM 147:3–4

God knows and numbers the stars, yet He is concerned about you and me, even though we're broken by sin. He binds our shattered hearts with sensitivity and kindness, and He brings healing into the depths of our souls. The greatness of God's power is the greatness of His heart. His strength is the measure of His love. He is a tender and mighty God.

The psalmist tells us that God "determines the number of the stars," and even "calls them each by name" (147:4). Would He care for the stars that are mere matter and not care for us, who bear His image? Of course not. He knows about our lonely struggles, and He cares. It is His business to care.

God, in the form of His Son Jesus, was subject to all our passions (Hebrews 2:18). He understands and does not scold or condemn when we fall short and fail. He leans down and listens to our cries for help. He gently corrects us. He heals through time and with great skill.

The stars will fall from the sky someday. They are not God's major concern—you are! He "is able to keep you from stumbling and to present you before his glorious presence without fault and with great joy" (Jude 1:24). And He will do it!

Because God cares about us,
we can leave our cares with Him.

How lovely is your dwelling place,
Lord Almighty!
My soul yearns, even faints,
for the courts of the Lord;
my heart and my flesh cry out
for the living God.
Even the sparrow has found a home,
and the swallow a nest for herself,
where she may have her young—
a place near your altar,
Lord Almighty, my King and my God.
Blessed are those who dwell in your house;
they are ever praising you.
Blessed are those whose strength is in you,
whose hearts are set on pilgrimage.
As they pass through the Valley of Baka,
they make it a place of springs;
the autumn rains also cover it with pools.
They go from strength to strength,
till each appears before God in Zion.
Hear my prayer, Lord God Almighty;
listen to me, God of Jacob.
Look on our shield, O God;
look with favor on your anointed one.
Better is one day in your courts
than a thousand elsewhere;
I would rather be a doorkeeper in the house of my God
than dwell in the tents of the wicked.
For the Lord God is a sun and shield;
the Lord bestows favor and honor;
no good thing does he withhold
from those whose walk is blameless.
Lord Almighty,
blessed is the one who trusts in you.

He Can Be Trusted

LORD *Almighty,*
blessed is the one who trusts in you.
—PSALM 84:12

I was sitting in my chair by the window, staring out through fir and spruce trees to the mountains beyond, lost in thought. I looked down and saw a young fox, staring up at my face. She was as still as a stone.

Days before, I had seen her at the edge of the woods, looking nervously over her shoulder at me. I went to the kitchen for an egg, and rolled it toward the place I had last seen her. Each day I put another egg on the lawn, and each day she ventured out of the trees just long enough to pick it up. Then she would dart back into the woods.

Now she had come on her own to my door to get an egg, convinced, I suppose, that I meant her no harm.

This incident reminded my wife of David's invitation: "Taste and see that the LORD is good" (Psalm 34:8). How do we start doing that? By taking in His Word. As we read and reflect on His compassion and lovingkindness, we learn that He can be trusted (84:12). We lose our dread of getting closer to Him. Our fear becomes a healthy respect and honor of Him.

You may at times distrust God, as the fox was wary of me at first. But give Him a chance to prove His love. Read about Jesus in the Gospels. Read the praises to God in the Psalms. Taste and see that He is good!

**No one is beyond the reach
of God's love.**

The waters saw you, God,
the waters saw you and writhed;
the very depths were convulsed.
The clouds poured down water,
the heavens resounded with thunder;
your arrows flashed back and forth.
Your thunder was heard in the whirlwind,
your lightning lit up the world;
the earth trembled and quaked.
Your path led through the sea,
your way through the mighty waters,
though your footprints were not seen.
You led your people like a flock
by the hand of Moses and Aaron.

Dangerous Crossings

Your path led through the sea,
your way through the mighty waters,
though your footprints were not seen.
—PSALM 77:19

I don't wade in swift streams anymore. The bottom's too slippery, the current's too strong, and my old legs aren't what they used to be.

So many challenges that I once took on readily are now too difficult for me. Like the psalmist, I lose sleep sometimes, wondering how I can negotiate them (Psalm 77:1–4).

Then I remember the "deeds of the LORD," His "miracles of long ago" (v. 11). His "path led through the sea, [His] way through mighty waters," though He left no footprints behind (v. 19).

That's the way it is with God. Although you can't see Him, He is surely there. Unseen, He leads His people "like a flock" (v. 20). He does not fear the currents and storms of life, for His strength and courage are infinite.

And there's more: The Shepherd leads us through the help of other people. He led Israel "by the hand of Moses and Aaron" (v. 20). He leads us in the wise counsel of a father or mother, in the strong grip of a godly friend, in the loving encouragement of a caring husband or wife, in the gentle touch of a young child.

Good hands are reaching out to us. Our Lord is a tough and tender Shepherd who leads through perilous crossings to the other side. Have you put your hand in His?

**God tells us to burden Him
with what burdens us.**

It is good to praise the LORD
and make music to your name, O Most High,
proclaiming your love in the morning
and your faithfulness at night,
to the music of the ten-stringed lyre
and the melody of the harp.
For you make me glad by your deeds, LORD;
I sing for joy at what your hands have done.
How great are your works, LORD,
how profound your thoughts!
Senseless people do not know,
fools do not understand,
that though the wicked spring up like grass
and all evildoers flourish,
they will be destroyed forever.
But you, LORD, are forever exalted.
For surely your enemies, LORD,
surely your enemies will perish;
all evildoers will be scattered.
You have exalted my horn like that of a wild ox;
fine oils have been poured on me.
My eyes have seen the defeat of my adversaries;
my ears have heard the rout of my wicked foes.
The righteous will flourish like a palm tree,
they will grow like a cedar of Lebanon;
planted in the house of the LORD,
they will flourish in the courts of our God.
They will still bear fruit in old age,
they will stay fresh and green,
proclaiming, "The LORD is upright;
he is my Rock, and there is no wickedness in him."

Planted in the House of the Lord

They will still bear fruit in old age,
they will stay fresh and green.
—PSALM 92:14

After conducting a series of interviews with elderly people, author Don Gold published the book *Until the Singing Stops: A Celebration of Life and Old Age in America.*

Gold loved and admired his grandmother, and it was the memory of her that moved him to meet and learn from other elderly people. He recalls that on the way to one of his interviews, he got lost on a dusty country road in Missouri. When he pulled into a farm to ask for directions, a teenager came up, listened, shrugged his shoulders, and then replied, "Don't know." So he drove on. A few miles farther down the road, he stopped again at a farmhouse. The farmer, who was an old man, graciously gave him flawless directions.

Perhaps, Gold mused, that experience sums up what he was searching for when the memory of his grandmother sent him out to find people like her. He was looking for someone to guide him in his life journey.

If you're "young," seek out older people who have been drinking deeply from God's love and goodness throughout their life. They have wisdom to share that will help you so that you also might flourish and grow in your faith (Psalm 92:12–14).

**Fellowship with Christ is the secret
of fruitfulness for Him.**

I lift up my eyes to you,
to you who sit enthroned in heaven.
As the eyes of slaves look to the hand of their master,
as the eyes of a female slave look to the hand of her mistress,
so our eyes look to the LORD our God,
till he shows us his mercy.
Have mercy on us, LORD, have mercy on us,
for we have endured no end of contempt.
We have endured no end
of ridicule from the arrogant,
of contempt from the proud.

Sticks and Stones

We have endured no end
of ridicule from the arrogant,
of contempt from the proud.
—PSALM 123:4

The psalmist was fed up with "the contempt from the proud" (Psalm 123:4). Perhaps you are too. People in your neighborhood, office, or classroom may be scornful of your faith and determination to follow Jesus. Sticks and stones do break our bones, but words can wound more deeply. In his commentary on this Psalm, Derek Kidner refers to contempt as "cold steel."

We can fend off the jeers of the proud by becoming like them, or we can view their attempt to humiliate us as a badge of honor. We can rejoice that we've been "counted worthy of suffering disgrace for [Jesus's name]" (Acts 5:41). Better to bear shame for a short time than to endure "everlasting contempt" (Daniel 12:2).

We must not be like the mockers by mocking them in turn, but bless those who persecute us. "Bless and do not curse," Paul reminds us (Romans 12:14). Then God may draw them to faith and repentance, and turn our moments of shame into eternal glory.

Finally, as the psalmist counsels us, we must "look to the LORD our God" (Psalm 123:2). He understands as no other, for He too has endured reproach. He will show compassion to us according to His infinite mercy.

When others' treatment
of you gets you down,
look up to Jesus.

I will exalt you, LORD,
for you lifted me out of the depths
and did not let my enemies gloat over me.
LORD my God, I called to you for help,
and you healed me.
You, LORD, brought me up from the realm of the dead;
you spared me from going down to the pit.
Sing the praises of the LORD, you his faithful people;
praise his holy name.
For his anger lasts only a moment,
but his favor lasts a lifetime;
weeping may stay for the night,
but rejoicing comes in the morning.
When I felt secure, I said,
"I will never be shaken."
LORD, when you favored me,
you made my royal mountain stand firm;
but when you hid your face,
I was dismayed.
To you, LORD, I called;
to the Lord I cried for mercy:
"What is gained if I am silenced,
if I go down to the pit?
Will the dust praise you?
Will it proclaim your faithfulness?
Hear, LORD, and be merciful to me;
LORD, be my help."
You turned my wailing into dancing;
you removed my sackcloth and clothed me with joy,
that my heart may sing your praises and not be silent.
LORD my God, I will praise you forever.

Sing to the Lord

Weeping may stay for the night,
but rejoicing comes in the morning.
—PSALM 30:5

It's as though a sinister stranger comes knocking on your door. You must let him in, for he knocks insistently and will not go away. He is sorrow personified.

You believe no one sees your tears and you feel all alone—but God sees them and He understands. "All night I flood my bed with weeping and drench my couch with tears," David said in Psalm 6:6. "The LORD has heard my weeping" (v. 8). "You number my wanderings; put my tears into Your bottle; are they not in Your book?" (56:8 NKJV). Though "weeping may stay for the night," it is a transient houseguest, for "rejoicing comes in the morning" (30:5).

We remember, as David did, that God's love and favor last for a lifetime. He has promised never to leave us nor forsake us. When God's love comes into our thoughts, our feelings of sorrow and dread flee. Our mourning is turned into dancing, our garments of sackcloth and sorrow are stripped away, and we are girded with gladness. We can rise to greet the day with shouts of ringing praise for His mercy, guidance, and protection. We rejoice in His holy name (30:11–12).

No matter our circumstances, let's sing to the Lord once again!

Praise is the voice
of a soul set free.

It is good to praise the LORD
and make music to your name, O Most High,
proclaiming your love in the morning
and your faithfulness at night,
to the music of the ten-stringed lyre
and the melody of the harp.
For you make me glad by your deeds, LORD;
I sing for joy at what your hands have done.
How great are your works, LORD,
how profound your thoughts!
Senseless people do not know,
fools do not understand,
that though the wicked spring up like grass
and all evildoers flourish,
they will be destroyed forever.
But you, LORD, are forever exalted.
For surely your enemies, LORD,
surely your enemies will perish;
all evildoers will be scattered.
You have exalted my horn like that of a wild ox;
fine oils have been poured on me.
My eyes have seen the defeat of my adversaries;
my ears have heard the rout of my wicked foes.
The righteous will flourish like a palm tree,
they will grow like a cedar of Lebanon;
planted in the house of the LORD,
they will flourish in the courts of our God.
They will still bear fruit in old age,
they will stay fresh and green,
proclaiming, "The LORD is upright;
he is my Rock, and there is no wickedness in him."

Give Thanks!

It is good to praise the LORD
and make music to your name,
O Most High.
—PSALM 92:1

Psalm 92 is a "Song for the Sabbath day," a resting place for those who are troubled.

The song begins with a commendation of praise: "It is good to praise the LORD." It does us good to turn from our unsettling and anxious thoughts to declare God's "love in the morning and [His] faithfulness at night" (v. 2). God loves us and is always faithful! He makes us glad (v. 4).

Praise not only makes us glad, it makes us wise. We begin to understand something of God's greatness and creative design in all that He does (vv. 5–9). We gain a wisdom that is hidden from those who do not know God. The wicked may "spring up like grass" for a moment, but ultimately they will "be destroyed" (v. 7).

The righteous, however, are joined to the One who is "forever exalted" (v. 8). They "flourish like a palm tree" and "like a cedar of Lebanon" (v. 12), symbols of graceful beauty and unbending strength. For they have been "planted in the house of the LORD" (v. 13). Their roots go down into the soil of God's faithfulness; they draw on His unquenchable love.

Give thanks and praise to the Lord today!

A heart in tune with God can't help
but sing His praises.

Praise the LORD, all you nations;
extol him, all you peoples.
For great is his love toward us,
and the faithfulness of the LORD endures forever.
Praise the LORD.

In Brief

For great is his love toward us.
—PSALM 117:2

I counted once and discovered that Abraham Lincoln's Gettysburg Address contains fewer than three hundred words. This means, among other things, that words don't have to be many to be memorable.

That's one reason I like Psalm 117. Brevity is its hallmark. The psalmist said all he had to say in thirty words (actually just seventeen words in the Hebrew text).

"Praise the LORD, all you Gentiles! Laud Him, all you peoples! For His merciful kindness [love] is great toward us, and the truth [faithfulness] of the LORD endures forever. Praise the LORD!" (NKJV).

Ah, that's the good news! Contained in this hallelujah Psalm is a message to all nations of the world that God's "merciful kindness"— His covenant love—is "great . . . toward us" (v. 2).

Think about what God's love means. God loved us before we were born; He will love us after we die. Not one thing can separate us from the love of God that is in Jesus our Lord (Romans 8:39). His heart is an inexhaustible and irrepressible fountain of love!

As I read this brief Psalm of praise to God, I can think of no greater encouragement for our journey than its reminder of God's merciful kindness. Praise the Lord!

**What we know about God should lead us
to give joyful praise to Him.**

Hasten, O God, to save me;
come quickly, Lord, to help me.
May those who want to take my life
be put to shame and confusion;
may all who desire my ruin
be turned back in disgrace.
May those who say to me, "Aha! Aha!"
turn back because of their shame.
But may all who seek you
rejoice and be glad in you;
may those who long for your saving help always say,
"The Lord is great!"
But as for me, I am poor and needy;
come quickly to me, O God.
You are my help and my deliverer;
Lord, do not delay.

Time to Pray?

*Come quickly,
LORD, to help me.*
—PSALM 70:1

One morning when I was a young child, I was sitting in the kitchen, watching my mother prepare breakfast. Suddenly, the grease in the skillet in which she was frying bacon caught fire. Flames shot into the air and my mother ran to the pantry for some baking soda to throw on the blaze.

"Help!" I shouted. And then I added, "Oh, I wish it was time to pray!" "It's time to pray" must have been a frequent household expression, and I took it quite literally to mean we could pray only at certain times.

The time to pray, of course, is any time—especially when we're in crisis. Fear, worry, anxiety, and care are the most common occasions for prayer. It is when we are desolate, forsaken, and stripped of every human resource that we naturally resort to prayer. We cry out with the words of David, "Come quickly, LORD, to help me" (Psalm 70:1).

John Cassian, a fifth-century Christian, wrote of this verse: "This is the terrified cry of someone who sees the snares of the enemy, the cry of someone besieged day and night and exclaiming that he cannot escape unless his Protector comes to the rescue."

May this be our simple prayer to the Lord in every crisis and all day long: "Help me!"

**There is no place or time
we cannot pray.**

I cry aloud to the LORD;
I lift up my voice to the LORD for mercy.
I pour out before him my complaint;
before him I tell my trouble.
When my spirit grows faint within me,
it is you who watch over my way.
In the path where I walk
people have hidden a snare for me.
Look and see, there is no one at my right hand;
no one is concerned for me.
I have no refuge;
no one cares for my life.
I cry to you, LORD;
I say, "You are my refuge,
my portion in the land of the living."
Listen to my cry,
for I am in desperate need;
rescue me from those who pursue me,
for they are too strong for me.
Set me free from my prison,
that I may praise your name.
Then the righteous will gather about me
because of your goodness to me.

Crying Out to God

By prayer and petition . . .
present your requests to God.
—PHILIPPIANS 4:6

After all these years, I still don't fully understand prayer. It's something of a mystery to me. But one thing I know: When we're in desperate need, prayer springs naturally from our lips and from the deepest level of our hearts.

When we're frightened out of our wits, when we're pushed beyond our limits, when we're pulled out of our comfort zones, when our well-being is challenged and endangered, we reflexively and involuntarily resort to prayer. "Help, Lord!" is our natural cry.

Author Eugene Peterson wrote: "The language of prayer is forged in the crucible of trouble. When we can't help ourselves and call for help, when we don't like where we are and want out, when we don't like who we are and want a change, we use primal language, and this language becomes the root language of prayer."

Prayer begins in trouble, and it continues because we're always in trouble at some level. It requires no special preparation, no precise vocabulary, no appropriate posture. It springs from us in the face of necessity and, in time, becomes our habitual response to every issue—good and bad—we face in this life (Philippians 4:6). What a privilege it is to carry everything to God in prayer!

**God's help is only
a prayer away.**

Lord, you are the God who saves me;
day and night I cry out to you.
May my prayer come before you;
turn your ear to my cry.
I am overwhelmed with troubles
and my life draws near to death.
I am counted among those who go down to the pit;
I am like one without strength.
I am set apart with the dead,
like the slain who lie in the grave,
whom you remember no more,
who are cut off from your care.
You have put me in the lowest pit,
in the darkest depths.
Your wrath lies heavily on me;
you have overwhelmed me with all your waves.
You have taken from me my closest friends
and have made me repulsive to them.
I am confined and cannot escape;
my eyes are dim with grief.
I call to you, Lord, every day;
I spread out my hands to you.

Do you show your wonders to the dead?
Do their spirits rise up and praise you?
Is your love declared in the grave,
your faithfulness in Destruction?
Are your wonders known in the place of darkness,
or your righteous deeds in the land of oblivion?
But I cry to you for help, Lord;
in the morning my prayer comes before you.
Why, Lord, do you reject me
and hide your face from me?
From my youth I have suffered and been close to death;
I have borne your terrors and am in despair.
Your wrath has swept over me;
your terrors have destroyed me.
All day long they surround me like a flood;
they have completely engulfed me.
You have taken from me friend and neighbor—
darkness is my closest friend.

Heman's Honesty

I am overwhelmed
with troubles.
—PSALM 88:3

I marvel at Heman, the poet who wrote Psalm 88. His lot in life was unrelieved distress. "I am overwhelmed with troubles," he lamented (v. 3). He was fed up with suffering!

Heman looked back and remembered poor health and misfortune. He looked around and saw adversity and abandonment. He looked up and found no solace. He was "in despair" he complained (v. 15). He was "cut off" (v. 5), "in the darkest depths" (v. 6), "overwhelmed" (v. 7), and feeling rejected (v. 14). He could see no light at the end of the tunnel; no resolution of his sorrow.

Heman's honesty warms my soul. Christians who never struggle confuse me. There's balance, of course: No one wants to be around those who babble on all day about their troubles, but it does my heart good to know that someone else has struggled.

Yet, there's more to Heman than mere candor. He also had a stubborn, intractable faith. Despite his many problems, he clung to God and cried out to Him "day and night" (v. 1). He didn't stop praying. He didn't give up. And even though he didn't sense it at the time, Heman acknowledged God's lovingkindness, faithfulness, and righteousness (vv. 11–12).

I like folks like Heman. They strengthen my grip on God and remind me never to stop praying.

**Prayer is the soil
in which hope grows best.**

Give thanks to the LORD, for he is good;
his love endures forever.
Let Israel say:
"His love endures forever."
Let the house of Aaron say:
"His love endures forever."
Let those who fear the LORD say:
"His love endures forever."
When hard pressed, I cried to the LORD;
he brought me into a spacious place.
The LORD is with me; I will not be afraid.
What can mere mortals do to me?
The LORD is with me; he is my helper.
I look in triumph on my enemies.
It is better to take refuge in the LORD
than to trust in humans.
It is better to take refuge in the LORD
than to trust in princes.
All the nations surrounded me,
but in the name of the LORD I cut them down.
They surrounded me on every side,
but in the name of the LORD I cut them down.
They swarmed around me like bees,
but they were consumed as quickly as burning thorns;
in the name of the LORD I cut them down.
I was pushed back and about to fall,
but the LORD helped me.
The LORD is my strength and my defense;
he has become my salvation.

continued . . .

Shouts of joy and victory
resound in the tents of the righteous:
"The Lord's right hand has done mighty things!
The Lord's right hand is lifted high;
the Lord's right hand has done mighty things!"
I will not die but live,
and will proclaim what the Lord has done.
The Lord has chastened me severely,
but he has not given me over to death.
Open for me the gates of the righteous;
I will enter and give thanks to the Lord.
This is the gate of the Lord
through which the righteous may enter.
I will give you thanks, for you answered me;
you have become my salvation.
The stone the builders rejected
has become the cornerstone;
the Lord has done this,
and it is marvelous in our eyes.
The Lord has done it this very day;
let us rejoice today and be glad.
Lord, save us!
Lord, grant us success!
Blessed is he who comes in the name of the Lord.
From the house of the Lord we bless you.
The Lord is God,
and he has made his light shine on us.
With boughs in hand, join in the festal procession
up to the horns of the altar.
You are my God, and I will praise you;
you are my God, and I will exalt you.
Give thanks to the Lord, for he is good;
his love endures forever.

Have a Great Day!

This is the day the LORD has made;
we will rejoice and be glad in it.
—PSALM 118:24 (NKJV)

I was in a convenience store one day, standing in line behind a man paying for his groceries. When he was finished, the clerk sent him off with a cheery "Have a great day!"

To the clerk's surprise (and mine) the man exploded in anger. "This is one of the worst days of my life," he shouted. "How can I have a great day?" And with that he stormed out of the store.

I understand the man's frustration; I too have "bad" days over which I have no control. How can I have a great day, I ask myself, when it's beyond my control? Then I remember these words: "This is the day the LORD has made" (Psalm 118:24 NKJV).

The Lord has made every day, and my Father will show himself strong on my behalf today. He has control over everything in it—even the hard things that will come my way. All events have been screened through His wisdom and love, and they are opportunities for me to grow in faith. "His love endures forever" (v. 1). "The LORD is with me; I will not be afraid" (v. 6).

Now, when people give me the parting admonition to have a great day, I reply, "That's beyond my control, but I can be grateful for whatever comes my way, and rejoice—for this is the day the Lord has made."

A smile is a curve that
can set things straight.

Where can I go from your Spirit?
Where can I flee from your presence?
If I go up to the heavens, you are there;
if I make my bed in the depths, you are there.
If I rise on the wings of the dawn,
if I settle on the far side of the sea,
even there your hand will guide me,
your right hand will hold me fast.
If I say, "Surely the darkness will hide me
and the light become night around me,"
even the darkness will not be dark to you;
the night will shine like the day,
for darkness is as light to you.

The Runaway Bunny

Where can I go from your Spirit?
Where can I flee from your presence?
—PSALM 139:7

Margaret Wise Brown is known for her simple yet profound books for children. One of my favorites is *The Runaway Bunny*. It's about a little bunny who tells his mother he has decided to run away.

"If you run away," says his mother, "I will run after you. For you are my little bunny." She goes on to tell him that if he becomes a fish in a trout stream, she will become a fisherman and fish for him. If he becomes a little boy, she will become a human mother and catch him in her arms and hug him. No matter what the little rabbit does, his doggedly persistent, ever-pursuing mother will not give up or go away.

"Shucks," says the bunny at last, "I might as well stay where I am and be your little bunny." "Have a carrot," his mother then says.

This story reminds me of David's words in Psalm 139:7–10, "Where can I go from your Spirit? Where can I flee from your presence? If I go up to the heavens, you are there; if I make my bed in the depths, you are there. If I rise on the wings of the dawn, if I settle on the far side of the sea, even there your hand will guide me, your right hand will hold me fast."

Let's be thankful that God is relentless in His love for us—ever-pursuing, ever-present, and ever-guiding.

> **No matter where you go,**
> **God goes with you.**

Refrain from anger and turn from wrath;
do not fret—it leads only to evil.
For those who are evil will be destroyed,
but those who hope in the LORD will inherit the land.
A little while, and the wicked will be no more;
though you look for them, they will not be found.
But the meek will inherit the land
and enjoy peace and prosperity.

Keep Me from Wrath

Refrain from anger
and turn from wrath.
—PSALM 37:8

I have a friend whose note cards are imprinted with a picture of Rodin's *The Thinker*, the famous sculpture depicting a man in sober reflection. Below the picture is this inscription: "Life is not fair."

Indeed, it is not. And any theory that insists that this life is fair is illusory and deceptive.

Despite the overwhelming unfairness of life, however, David in Psalm 37 prays that he will not retaliate but will instead rest in the Lord and wait patiently for Him to bring justice to the earth in due time (v. 7). "For those who are evil will be destroyed, but those who hope in the LORD will inherit the land" (v. 9).

Our wrath tends to be vindictive and punitive. God's wrath is untainted by self-interest and tempered by mercy. His wrath can even be His relentless love that brings our antagonists to repentance and faith. We must not then avenge ourselves, "for it is written, 'It is mine to avenge; I will repay,' says the Lord. . . . Do not be overcome by evil, but overcome evil with good" (Romans 12:19, 21).

This must begin in the heart, the wellspring from which the issues of our lives flow. May we cease from anger, forsake wrath, and wait patiently for the Lord.

**Revenge restrained
is a victory gained.**

Praise the LORD, all you servants of the LORD
who minister by night in the house of the LORD.
Lift up your hands in the sanctuary
and praise the LORD.
May the LORD bless you from Zion,
he who is the Maker of heaven and earth.

A Voice in the Night

Lift up your hands in the sanctuary
and praise the LORD!
—PSALM 134:2

Psalm 134 has only three verses, but it is proof that little things can mean a lot. The first two verses are an admonition to the priests who serve in God's house night after night. The building was dark and empty; nothing of consequence was occurring—or so it seemed. Yet these ministers were encouraged to "lift up your hands in the sanctuary and praise the LORD!" (v. 2). The third verse is a voice from the congregation calling into the darkness and loneliness of the night: "The LORD . . . is the maker of heaven and earth."

I think of other servants of the Lord today—pastors and their families who serve in small churches in small places. They're often discouraged, tempted to lose heart, doing their best, serving unnoticed and unrewarded. They wonder if anyone cares what they're doing; if anyone ever thinks of them, prays for them, or considers them a part of their lives.

I would say to them—and to anyone who is feeling lonely or insignificant: Though your place is small, it is a holy place. The one who made and moves heaven and earth is at work in and through you. "Lift up your hands" and praise Him.

Anyone doing God's work in God's way
is important in His sight.

In you, Lord my God,
I put my trust.
I trust in you;
do not let me be put to shame,
nor let my enemies triumph over me.
No one who hopes in you
will ever be put to shame,
but shame will come on those
who are treacherous without cause.
Show me your ways, Lord,
teach me your paths.
Guide me in your truth and teach me,
for you are God my Savior,
and my hope is in you all day long.
Remember, Lord, your great mercy and love,
for they are from of old.
Do not remember the sins of my youth
and my rebellious ways;
according to your love remember me,
for you, Lord, are good.
Good and upright is the Lord;
therefore he instructs sinners in his ways.
He guides the humble in what is right
and teaches them his way.
All the ways of the Lord are loving and faithful
toward those who keep the demands of his covenant.
For the sake of your name, Lord,
forgive my iniquity, though it is great.

Revealed to Be Healed

Show me your ways, LORD,
teach me your paths.
—PSALM 25:4

As a boy, I watched my father plow fields that had never been cultivated. On the first pass the plowshare would turn up large rocks, which he hauled away. Then he would plow the field again, and then again, to further break up the soil. With each pass the plow turned up other, smaller rocks that he cast aside. The process continued, requiring many passes through the field.

Growth in grace can look like a similar process. When we first become believers, some "big" sins may be exposed. We confess them to God and accept His forgiveness. But as the years pass by, and as God's Word passes through us and sinks into our innermost being, the Holy Spirit brings other sins to the surface. Sins of the spirit once thought to be mere peccadilloes—small, seemingly unimportant offenses—are revealed as ugly, ruinous attitudes and actions. These are sins like pride, self-pity, complaining, pettiness, prejudice, spite, self-serving indulgence.

God reveals each sin so He can cast it aside. He reveals to heal. When harmful hidden attitudes come to the surface, we can pray as the psalmist David did, "For the sake of your name, LORD, forgive my iniquity, though it is great" (Psalm 25:11).

Humbling exposure, though painful, is good for the soul. It's one of the ways in which He "instructs sinners in his ways." He "guides the humble in what is right and teaches them his way" (vv. 8–9).

**Jesus takes us as we are and
makes us what we should be.**

PSALM 51:9–13

Hide your face from my sins
and blot out all my iniquity.
Create in me a pure heart, O God,
and renew a steadfast spirit within me.
Do not cast me from your presence
or take your Holy Spirit from me.
Restore to me the joy of your salvation
and grant me a willing spirit, to sustain me.
Then I will teach transgressors your ways,
so that sinners will turn back to you.

Better Than Ever

Restore to me the joy of your salvation
and grant me a willing spirit, to sustain me.
—PSALM 51:12

The story is told of a group of salmon fishermen who gathered in a Scottish inn after a long day of fishing. As one was describing a catch to his friends, his arm swept across the table and knocked a glass against the wall, shattering it and leaving a stain on the white plaster surface. The man apologized to the innkeeper and offered to pay for the damage, but there was nothing he could do; the wall was ruined. A man seated nearby said, "Don't worry." Rising, he took a painting implement from his pocket and began to sketch around the ugly stain. Slowly there emerged the head of a magnificent stag. The man was Sir E. H. Landseer, Scotland's foremost animal artist.

David, Israel's illustrious king who penned Psalm 51, brought shame on himself and his nation by his sins. He committed adultery with the wife of one of his friends and engineered the death of that friend—both deeds worthy of death. It would seem his life was ruined. But he pled with God: "Restore to me the joy of your salvation and grant me a willing spirit, to sustain me" (v. 12).

Like David we have shameful acts in our past and the memories that accompany them, recollections that taunt us in the middle of the night. There's so much we wish we could undo or redo.

There is a grace that not only forgives sin but also uses it to make us better than before. God wastes nothing.

God has both an all-seeing eye
and all-forgiving heart.

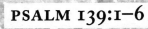
You have searched me, LORD,
and you know me.
You know when I sit and when I rise;
you perceive my thoughts from afar.
You discern my going out and my lying down;
you are familiar with all my ways.
Before a word is on my tongue
you, LORD, know it completely.
You hem me in behind and before,
and you lay your hand upon me.
Such knowledge is too wonderful for me,
too lofty for me to attain.

Informing God

*Can anyone teach
knowledge to God?*
—JOB 21:22

We cannot tell God anything He doesn't already know. When we pray, we simply put into words what He's been aware of all along.

That doesn't make prayer unnecessary; rather, it encourages us to pray. We find relief in talking to Someone who knows us and our situation fully. It's a comfort to know that God's response arises not from information we give Him but from His perfect knowledge of our circumstances. He knows all conditions—past, present, and future—that bear on our well-being.

"Your Father knows," Jesus said in Matthew 6:8. He knows our thoughts, our intentions, our desires; He is intimately acquainted with all our ways (Psalm 139:3). He knows the anguish of our heart, the strain of continual frustration, the enemies inside and outside that war against our souls.

So, can we presume to dictate the time and terms of our deliverance from trials or adversity? Can we say our way is better, more likely to develop our soul? No, we cannot teach God anything. He alone knows the way to bring us to glory. Out of all possible paths, He has chosen the best, the route most adapted to who we are and what He has in store for us.

We cannot teach God knowledge, but we can love and trust Him. That's all He asks of us.

**God knows the end from the beginning,
so we can trust Him
with everything between.**

Show me your ways, Lord,
teach me your paths.
Guide me in your truth and teach me,
for you are God my Savior,
and my hope is in you all day long.
Remember, Lord, your great mercy and love,
for they are from of old.
Do not remember the sins of my youth
and my rebellious ways;
according to your love remember me,
for you, Lord, are good.
Good and upright is the Lord;
therefore he instructs sinners in his ways.
He guides the humble in what is right
and teaches them his way.
All the ways of the Lord are loving and faithful
toward those who keep the demands of his covenant.
For the sake of your name, Lord,
forgive my iniquity, though it is great.

The Rugged Road

"Ask where the good way is, and walk in it,
and you will find rest for your souls."
—JEREMIAH 6:16

A fishing buddy of mine told me about an alpine lake located high on the north flank of Jughandle Mountain here in Idaho. Rumor had it that large cutthroat trout lurked up there. My friend got a pencil and scrap of napkin and drew a map for me. Several weeks later I gassed up my truck and set out to follow his directions.

His map put me on one of the worst roads I've ever driven! It was an old logging road that had been bulldozed through the forest and never regraded. Washouts, fallen timber, deep ruts, and large rocks battered my spine and bent the undercarriage of my truck. It took half a morning to reach my destination, and when I finally arrived I asked myself, "Why would a *friend* send me up a road like this?"

But the lake was magnificent and the fish were indeed large and scrappy! My friend had put me on the right road—one I would have chosen myself and patiently endured had I known what I knew at the end.

There is a faithful saying: "All the ways of the LORD are loving and faithful toward those who keep the demands of his covenant" (Psalm 25:10). Some of God's paths for us are rough and rugged; others, tedious and boring, but all are filled with His love and faithfulness. When we come to the end of our journey and know what we then will know, we will say, "God's path was best for me."

Our path may have obstacles,
but God will lead us.

Shout for joy to God, all the earth!
Sing the glory of his name;
make his praise glorious.
Say to God, "How awesome are your deeds!
So great is your power
that your enemies cringe before you.
All the earth bows down to you;
they sing praise to you,
they sing the praises of your name."
Come and see what God has done,
his awesome deeds for mankind!
He turned the sea into dry land,
they passed through the waters on foot—
come, let us rejoice in him.
He rules forever by his power,
his eyes watch the nations—
let not the rebellious rise up against him.
Praise our God, all peoples,
let the sound of his praise be heard;
he has preserved our lives
and kept our feet from slipping.
For you, God, tested us;
you refined us like silver.
You brought us into prison
and laid burdens on our backs.
You let people ride over our heads;
we went through fire and water,
but you brought us to a place of abundance.

Tried by Fire

You, God, have tested us;
you refined us like silver.
—PSALM 66:10

"The main end of life is not to do but to become," said respected British pastor F. B. Meyer (1847–1929). And for this we are being prepared every day. As silver is refined by fire, the heart is often refined in the furnace of sadness. The psalmist said in his sorrow, "We went through fire" (Psalm 66:12).

The refining process may be very painful, but it will not destroy us, for the Refiner sits by the furnace tending the flame. He will not allow us to be tried beyond our endurance; it is for our good.

We may not understand why we have to endure such misery year after year. The ordeal seems endless and pointless. Our days are wasted, or so it appears. We feel as if we are doing nothing of lasting significance.

But God is doing what matters—we are being refined. He is placing us into a crucible in which we acquire patience, meekness, humility, compassion, and the other "quiet" virtues our souls naturally lack.

So don't be afraid and don't fret. Your present trial, as painful as it may be, has been screened through God's wisdom and love. The Refiner sits beside the crucible tempering the flames, monitoring the process, waiting patiently until His face is mirrored in the surface.

The fires of testing can produce
a shining testimony.

I cry aloud to the LORD;
I lift up my voice to the LORD for mercy.
I pour out before him my complaint;
before him I tell my trouble.
When my spirit grows faint within me,
it is you who watch over my way.
In the path where I walk
people have hidden a snare for me.
Look and see, there is no one at my right hand;
no one is concerned for me.
I have no refuge;
no one cares for my life.
I cry to you, LORD;
I say, "You are my refuge,
my portion in the land of the living."
Listen to my cry,
for I am in desperate need;
rescue me from those who pursue me,
for they are too strong for me.
Set me free from my prison,
that I may praise your name.
Then the righteous will gather about me
because of your goodness to me.

A Long and Winding Path

When my spirit grows faint within me,
it is you who watch over my way.
In the path where I walk
people have hidden a snare for me.
—PSALM 142:3

Sometimes the path of life seems impossibly steep and lengthy. I have no strength and no will for the journey. Then I remember God knew this path long before I was called to walk it. He has always known the difficulties I would experience, the pain that I could never explain to another. He knows and offers His presence.

Perhaps you're overwhelmed with sadness today. It may be the weight of a difficult ministry; the worry of a hard marriage; the sorrow of a struggling child; the care of an aging parent; other troubles that come with life. "Surely," you say, "God would not have me walk this way. There must be another, easier path for me to travel."

But are any of us wise enough to know that some other way would make us into better and wiser children? No, our Father in heaven knows the best path, out of all possible paths, to bring us to completion (Psalm 142:3).

His ways are higher than our ways; His thoughts higher than our thoughts (Isaiah 55:9). We can humbly take the path He has marked out for us today and do so in absolute trust in His infinite wisdom and love. He is wiser and more loving than we can ever know. He who sees has foreseen and will not lead us astray.

**God will never lead you
down a wrong path.**

I waited patiently for the LORD;
he turned to me and heard my cry.
He lifted me out of the slimy pit,
out of the mud and mire;
he set my feet on a rock
and gave me a firm place to stand.
He put a new song in my mouth,
a hymn of praise to our God.
Many will see and fear the LORD
and put their trust in him.

The Discipline of Waiting

I waited patiently for the LORD;
he turned to me and heard my cry.
—PSALM 40:1

Waiting is hard. We wait in grocery lines, in traffic, in the doctor's office. We twiddle our thumbs, stifle our yawns, and fret inwardly in frustration. On another level, we wait for a letter that doesn't come, for a prodigal child to return, or for a spouse to change. We wait for a child we can hold in our arms. We wait for our heart's desire.

In Psalm 40, David says, "I waited patiently for the LORD" (v. 1). The original language here suggests that David "waited and waited and waited" for God to answer his prayer. Yet as he looks back at this time of delay, he praises God. As a result, David says, God "put a new song . . . a hymn of praise" in his heart (40:3).

"What a chapter can be written of God's delays!" said F. B. Meyer. "It is the mystery of educating human spirits to the finest temper of which they are capable." Through the discipline of waiting, we can develop the quieter virtues—submission, humility, patience, joyful endurance, persistence in well-doing—virtues that take the longest to learn.

What do we do when God seems to withhold our heart's desire? He is able to help us to love and trust Him enough to accept the delay with joy and to see it as an opportunity to develop these virtues—and to praise Him.

Waiting for God
is never a waste of time.

PSALM 131

My heart is not proud, Lord,
my eyes are not haughty;
I do not concern myself with great matters
or things too wonderful for me.
But I have calmed and quieted myself,
I am like a weaned child with its mother;
like a weaned child I am content.
Israel, put your hope in the Lord
both now and forevermore.

Why Me?

Recently I read Psalm 131, one of my favorite Psalms. In the past, I viewed it as an encouragement to understand that mystery is one of the hallmarks of God's character. It challenged me to let my mind be at rest, since I am unable to understand all that God is doing in His universe.

But then I saw another side of David's calm spirit: I am unable to understand all that God is doing in me, and it is impossible to try.

David draws a comparison between a weaned child who no longer frets for what it once demanded and a soul that has learned the same lesson. It is a call to learn humility, patient endurance, and contentment in all my circumstances—whatever they are—though I do not understand God's reasons. Divine logic is beyond the grasp of my mind.

I ask, "Why this affliction? Why this anguish?" The Father answers, "Hush, child. You wouldn't understand if I explained it to you. Just trust Me!"

So, I turn from contemplating David's example to ask myself: Can I, in my circumstances, "hope in the LORD"? (v. 3). Can I wait in faith and patience without fretting and without questioning God's wisdom? Can I trust Him while He works in me His good, acceptable, and perfect will?

**In a world of mystery,
it's a comfort to know the God
who knows all things.**

I will extol the LORD at all times;
his praise will always be on my lips.
I will glory in the LORD;
let the afflicted hear and rejoice.
Glorify the LORD with me;
let us exalt his name together.
I sought the LORD, and he answered me;
he delivered me from all my fears.
Those who look to him are radiant;
their faces are never covered with shame.
This poor man called, and the LORD heard him;
he saved him out of all his troubles.
The angel of the LORD encamps around those who fear him,
and he delivers them.
Taste and see that the LORD is good;
blessed is the one who takes refuge in him.
Fear the LORD, you his holy people,
for those who fear him lack nothing.
The lions may grow weak and hungry,
but those who seek the LORD lack no good thing.
Come, my children, listen to me;
I will teach you the fear of the LORD.
Whoever of you loves life
and desires to see many good days,
keep your tongue from evil
and your lips from telling lies.
Turn from evil and do good;
seek peace and pursue it.

An Enduring Happiness

Whoever of you loves life and
desires to see many good days. . . .
Turn from evil and do good.
—PSALM 34:12, 14

Often we hear that happiness comes from doing things our own way. That, however, is not true. That philosophy leads only to emptiness, anxiety, and heartache.

Poet W. H. Auden observed people as they attempted to find an escape in pleasures. He wrote of such people: "Lost in a haunted wood, / Children afraid of the night / Who have never been happy or good."

The psalmist David sings of the remedy for our fears and unhappiness. "I sought the LORD, and he answered me; he delivered me from all my fears" (Psalm 34:4). Happiness is doing things God's way, a fact that can be verified every day. "Those who look to him are radiant," writes David (v. 5). Just try it and you'll see. That's what he means when he says, "Taste and see that the LORD is good" (v. 8).

We say, "Seeing is believing." That's how we know things in this world. Show me proof and I'll believe it. God puts it the other way around. Believing is seeing. "Taste and then you will see."

Take the Lord at His word. Do the very next thing He is asking you to do and you will see. He will give you grace to do the right thing and more: He will give you himself—the only source of goodness—and with it, enduring happiness.

> **Happiness is doing**
> **the right thing.**

Hasten, O God, to save me;
come quickly, Lord, to help me.
May those who want to take my life
be put to shame and confusion;
may all who desire my ruin
be turned back in disgrace.
May those who say to me, "Aha! Aha!"
turn back because of their shame.
But may all who seek you
rejoice and be glad in you;
may those who long for your saving help always say,
"The Lord is great!"
But as for me, I am poor and needy;
come quickly to me, O God.
You are my help and my deliverer;
Lord, do not delay.

The Waiting Place

Be still before the LORD and wait patiently for him;
do not fret when people succeed in their ways,
when they carry out their wicked schemes.
—PSALM 37:7

"Waiting for the fish to bite or waiting for wind to fly a kite. Or waiting around for Friday night. . . . Everyone is just waiting"—or so Dr. Seuss, author of many children's books, says.

So much of life is about waiting, but God is never in a hurry—or so it seems. "God has His hour and delay," suggests an old, reliable saying. Thus we wait.

Waiting is hard. We twiddle our thumbs, shuffle our feet, stifle our yawns, heave long sighs, and fret inwardly in frustration. Why must I live with this awkward person, this tedious job, this embarrassing behavior, this health issue that will not go away? Why doesn't God come through?

God's answer: "Wait awhile and see what I will do."

Waiting is one of life's best teachers for in it we learn the virtue of . . . well, waiting—waiting while God works in us and for us. It's in waiting that we develop endurance, the ability to trust God's love and goodness, even when things aren't going our way (Psalm 70:5).

But waiting is not dreary, teeth-clenched resignation. We can "rejoice and be glad in [Him]" while we wait (v. 4). We wait in hope, knowing that God will deliver us in due time—in this world or in the next. God is never in a hurry, but He's always on time.

**God is with us
in our waiting.**

Oh, how I love your law!
I meditate on it all day long.
Your commands are always with me
and make me wiser than my enemies.
I have more insight than all my teachers,
for I meditate on your statutes.
I have more understanding than the elders,
for I obey your precepts.
I have kept my feet from every evil path
so that I might obey your word.
I have not departed from your laws,
for you yourself have taught me.
How sweet are your words to my taste,
sweeter than honey to my mouth!
I gain understanding from your precepts;
therefore I hate every wrong path.

The Goodness
of the Lord

Oh, how I love your law!
—PSALM 119:97

Some years ago I came across a short essay written by Sir James Barrie, an English baron. In it he gives an intimate picture of his mother, who deeply loved God and His Word, and who literally read her Bible to pieces. "It is mine now," Sir James wrote, "and to me the black threads with which she stitched it are a part of the contents."

My mother also loved God's Word. She read and pondered it for sixty years or more. I keep her Bible on my bookshelf in a prominent place. It too is tattered and torn, each stained page marked with her comments and reflections. As a boy, I often walked into her room in the morning and found her cradling her Bible in her lap, poring over its words. She did so until the day she could no longer see the words on the page. Even then her Bible was the most precious book in her possession.

When Sir James's mother grew old, she could no longer read the words of her Bible. Yet daily, her husband put her Bible in her hands, and she would reverently hold it there.

The psalmist wrote, "How sweet are your words to my taste, sweeter than honey to my mouth!" (119:103). Have you tasted the goodness of the Lord? Open your Bible today.

> **A well-read Bible is
> a sign of a well-fed soul.**

When you, God, went out before your people,
when you marched through the wilderness,
the earth shook, the heavens poured down rain,
before God, the One of Sinai,
before God, the God of Israel.
You gave abundant showers, O God;
you refreshed your weary inheritance.
Your people settled in it,
and from your bounty, God, you provided for the poor. . . .
Praise be to the Lord, to God our Savior,
who daily bears our burdens.
Our God is a God who saves;
from the Sovereign Lord comes escape from death.

Hoo-ah!

Blessed be the Lord,
who daily loads us with benefits,
the God of our salvation! Selah.
—PSALM 68:19 (NKJV)

The US Army's expression "hoo-ah" is a guttural response barked when troops voice approval. Its original meaning is lost to history, but some say it is derived from an old acronym HUA—Heard, Understood, and Acknowledged. I first heard the word in basic training.

Many years later it found its way into my vocabulary again when I began to meet on Wednesday mornings with a group of men to study the Scriptures. One morning one of the men—a former member of the 82nd Airborne Division—was reading one of the Psalms and came to the notation *selah* that occurs throughout the Psalms. Instead of reading *"selah,"* however, he growled *hoo-ah*, and that became our word for *selah* ever after.

No one knows for certain what *selah* actually means. Some say it is only a musical notation. It often appears after a truth that calls for a deep-seated, emotional response. In that sense *hoo-ah* works for me.

This morning I read Psalm 68:19: "Blessed be the Lord, who daily [day to day] loads us with benefits, the God of our salvation! Selah" (NKJV).

Imagine that! Every single morning God loads us up on His shoulders and carries us through the day. *He* is our salvation. Thus safe and secure in Him, we've no cause for worry or for fear.

"Hoo-ah!" I say.

> **Worship is giving God the best**
> **that He has given you.**
> —OSWALD CHAMBERS

Do not be far from me, my God;
come quickly, God, to help me.
May my accusers perish in shame;
may those who want to harm me
be covered with scorn and disgrace.
As for me, I will always have hope;
I will praise you more and more.
My mouth will tell of your righteous deeds,
of your saving acts all day long—
though I know not how to relate them all.
I will come and proclaim your mighty acts, Sovereign LORD;
I will proclaim your righteous deeds, yours alone.
Since my youth, God, you have taught me,
and to this day I declare your marvelous deeds.
Even when I am old and gray,
do not forsake me, my God,
till I declare your power to the next generation,
your mighty acts to all who are to come.

Pass It On

When I am old and gray,
do not forsake me, my God,
till I declare your power
to the next generation.
—PSALM 71:18

Getting older doesn't mean becoming obsolete. It can mean growing, maturing, serving, ministering, venturing, enjoying ourselves to the end of our days. "Old men ought to be explorers," author T. S. Eliot said. One of my friends says, "Have a blast while you last."

To idle away our last years is to rob ourselves of what could be the best years of our lives and to deprive the church of gifts God has given to enrich it. There is still service to be rendered and there are victories to be won.

Some older folks may not have the energy or inclination for leadership, but they are an invaluable asset to the next generation of leaders. John Wesley was asked what he would do if he knew he had only a short time to live. He responded, "I should meet with my young men till the moment came that I was called to yield my spirit back to Him that gave it."

The psalmist also desired to pass along his understanding of the Lord to others, and he prayed, "When I am old and gray, do not forsake me, my God, till I declare your power to the next generation" (Psalm 71:18).

We too should remain open to being used by God to enrich others' lives. Our greatest usefulness may be to pass our understanding of God on to others.

> To forget the elderly is to ignore
> the wisdom of the years.

Yet I am always with you;
you hold me by my right hand.
You guide me with your counsel,
and afterward you will take me into glory.
Whom have I in heaven but you?
And earth has nothing I desire besides you.
My flesh and my heart may fail,
but God is the strength of my heart
and my portion forever.
Those who are far from you will perish;
you destroy all who are unfaithful to you.
But as for me, it is good to be near God.
I have made the Sovereign LORD my refuge;
I will tell of all your deeds.

My Staff

By faith Jacob . . .
worshiped as he leaned
on the top of his staff.
—HEBREWS 11:21

An antique rack in the entryway to our home holds the canes and walking sticks of several generations of our family. My favorite is a slender staff with a gold-plated knob engraved with the initials "DHR." It belonged to my wife Carolyn's great-grandfather, Daniel Henry Rankin. Curiously, his initials are the same as mine.

In my study is another collection: my father's peeled, applewood walking stick, among others. And in a barrel in our garage there's an assortment of cross-country ski poles, wading wands, and trekking sticks I've gathered over the years. One of these days, I'll trade them all in for a walker. I'll always need something or someone to lean on.

I'm reminded of the old patriarch Jacob, once strong, now humbled and utterly dependent on God. When he was dying, by faith he "worshiped as he leaned on the top of his staff" (Hebrews 11:21).

As I grow older, I'm learning to lean more on God and His faithfulness. Over the years, He has held "me by my right hand." He is guiding me with His counsel, and afterward He will "take me into glory" (Psalm 73:23–24).

Shakespeare said it well: God is "the very staff of my age, my very prop."

**Learning of our weakness teaches us
to lean on God's strength.**

Lord, how many are my foes!
How many rise up against me!
Many are saying of me,
"God will not deliver him."
But you, Lord, are a shield around me,
my glory, the One who lifts my head high.
I call out to the Lord,
and he answers me from his holy mountain.
I lie down and sleep;
I wake again, because the Lord sustains me.
I will not fear though tens of thousands
assail me on every side.
Arise, Lord!
Deliver me, my God!
Strike all my enemies on the jaw;
break the teeth of the wicked.
From the Lord comes deliverance.
May your blessing be on your people.

God, My Glory

But you, LORD,
are a shield around me,
my glory, the One
who lifts my head high.
—PSALM 3:3

Is God your glory? (Psalm 3:3). The word *glory* is the translation of a Hebrew word meaning "weight" or "significance."

Some people measure their worth by beauty, intelligence, money, power, or prestige. But David, who wrote Psalm 3, found his security and worth in God. He said that many stood against him. He heard their cruel voices and was tempted to believe them, to give way to discouragement and depression. Nevertheless, he comforted and strengthened his heart with these words: "You, LORD, are a shield around me, my glory, the One who lifts my head high" (v. 3).

What a change that realization made! He had God, and his enemies did not. So he could hold up his head with confidence.

Verses like Psalm 3:3 can bring peace to your heart even in the midst of a storm of trouble. God is your shield and deliverer. He will deal with your adversaries in due time.

Meanwhile, tell God all about your troubles. Let Him be your glory. You don't have to defend yourself. Ask Him to be your shield— to protect your heart with His overshadowing love and care. Then, like David, you can lie down in peace and sleep, though tens of thousands are against you (vv. 5–6).

No one is more secure than the one
who is held in God's hands.

The righteous will flourish like a palm tree,
they will grow like a cedar of Lebanon;
planted in the house of the LORD,
they will flourish in the courts of our God.
They will still bear fruit in old age,
they will stay fresh and green,
proclaiming, "The LORD is upright;
he is my Rock, and there is no wickedness in him."

What We Cannot Lose

Even to your old age and gray hairs I am he,
I am he who will sustain you.
I have made you and I will carry you;
I will sustain you and I will rescue you.

—ISAIAH 46:4

Years ago I heard about an elderly gentleman who was suffering from the first stages of dementia. He lamented the fact that he often forgot about God. "Don't you worry," said a good friend, "He will never forget you."

Growing old is perhaps the hardest task we have to face in this life. As the saying goes, "Getting old is not for sissies."

Mainly, growing old is about losses. We devote most of our early life to acquiring things, but they are merely things we will lose as we age. We lose our strength, our looks, our friends, our job. We may lose our wealth, our home, our health, our spouse, our independence, and perhaps the greatest loss of all, our sense of dignity and self-worth.

But there is one thing that you and I will never lose—the love of God. "Even to your old age and gray hairs I am he," God said to the prophet, "I am he who will sustain you. I have made you and I will carry you; I will sustain you and I will rescue you" (Isaiah 46:4).

"The righteous will flourish like a palm tree," wrote the songwriter (Psalm 92:12). Those who are "planted in the house of the LORD, they will flourish in the courts of our God. They shall still bear fruit in old age" (vv. 13–14).

> God's love
> never grows old.

Unless the LORD builds the house,
the builders labor in vain.
Unless the LORD watches over the city,
the guards stand watch in vain.
In vain you rise early
and stay up late,
toiling for food to eat—
for he grants sleep to those he loves.
Children are a heritage from the LORD,
offspring a reward from him.
Like arrows in the hands of a warrior
are children born in one's youth.
Blessed is the man
whose quiver is full of them.
They will not be put to shame
when they contend with their opponents in court.

Legacy

*Children are a heritage
from the LORD.*
—PSALM 127:3

A friend of mine wrote recently, "If we died tomorrow, the company that we are working for could easily replace us in a matter of days. But the family left behind would feel the loss for the rest of their lives. Why then do we invest so much in our work and so little in our children's lives?"

Why do we sometimes exhaust ourselves rising up early and going late to rest, "eating the bread of anxious toil" (Psalm 127:1–2 ESV), busying ourselves to make our mark on this world, and overlooking the one investment that matters beyond everything else—our children?

Solomon declared, "Children are a heritage from the LORD"—an invaluable legacy He has bequeathed us. "Like arrows in the hand of a warrior, so are the children of one's youth" (v. 4 NKJV) is his striking simile. Nothing is more worthy of our energy and time.

There is no need for "anxious toil," working night and day, the wise man Solomon proclaimed, for the Lord does take care of us (Psalm 127:2). We can make time for our children and trust that the Lord will provide for all of our physical needs. Children, whether our own or those we disciple, are our lasting legacy—an investment we'll never regret.

**Time spent with your children
is time wisely invested.**

Be merciful to me, my God,
for my enemies are in hot pursuit;
all day long they press their attack.
My adversaries pursue me all day long;
in their pride many are attacking me.
When I am afraid, I put my trust in you.
In God, whose word I praise—
in God I trust and am not afraid.
What can mere mortals do to me?
All day long they twist my words;
all their schemes are for my ruin.
They conspire, they lurk,
they watch my steps,
hoping to take my life.
Because of their wickedness do not let them escape;
in your anger, God, bring the nations down.
Record my misery;
list my tears on your scroll—
are they not in your record?
Then my enemies will turn back
when I call for help.
By this I will know that God is for me.
In God, whose word I praise,
in the LORD, whose word I praise—
in God I trust and am not afraid.
What can man do to me?
I am under vows to you, my God;
I will present my thank offerings to you.
For you have delivered me from death
and my feet from stumbling,
that I may walk before God
in the light of life.

When I'm Afraid

When I am afraid,
I put my trust in you.
—PSALM 56:3

David fled from the home of the priests in Nob with Saul in hot pursuit. He made his way to Gath, the home of his enemies, where he was instantly recognized and brought before King Achish.

David's fame was celebrated everywhere in story and song. He had slain thousands of Philistines (1 Samuel 21:11), a reputation established at the expense of bereaved Philistine women and children. Here was an opportunity to take revenge.

David lost his nerve. In terror, he "pretended to be insane . . . , making marks on the doors of the gate and letting saliva run down his beard" (v. 13). Achish dismissed him with contempt: "Must this man come into my house?" (v. 15). Broken and utterly humiliated, David fled to Adullam in Judah. Close by was a hill honeycombed with caves. Into one of those holes he crept—alone.

As he experienced the solitude of that cave, at the nadir of his life and surrounded by enemies, David began to reflect on God's tender, faithful love. "When I am afraid, I put my trust in you," he wrote (Psalm 56:3). "You number my wanderings; put my tears into Your bottle" (v. 8 NKJV).

Perhaps you're "in a cave" today. You too can say, "In God I trust and am not afraid. What can man do to me?" (v. 11).

Loneliness is being unaware of the One
who is with us everywhere.

Out of the depths I cry to you, Lord;
Lord, hear my voice.
Let your ears be attentive
to my cry for mercy.
If you, Lord, kept a record of sins,
Lord, who could stand?
But with you there is forgiveness,
so that we can, with reverence, serve you.
I wait for the Lord, my whole being waits,
and in his word I put my hope.
I wait for the Lord
more than watchmen wait for the morning,
more than watchmen wait for the morning.
Israel, put your hope in the Lord,
for with the Lord is unfailing love
and with him is full redemption.
He himself will redeem Israel
from all their sins.

No Record of Our Sins

If you, LORD, kept a record of sins,
Lord, who could stand?
—PSALM 130:3

"Out of the depths" the psalmist cries to God (Psalm 130:1). His problem surfaces: terrible guilt for things done and undone in the past. "If you, LORD, kept a record of sins, Lord, who could stand?" (v. 3).

But, thankfully, God forgives. He does not keep an account of past sins, no matter how many or how grievous they have been. "Therefore, there is now no condemnation for those who are in Christ Jesus" (Romans 8:1). God's forgiveness then leads us to serve Him (Psalm 130:4). We worship and adore God, for grace and forgiveness cause us to love Him all the more.

But what happens if we slide back into old sins? What if sin lingers? We are to repent and "wait for the LORD" (v. 5). And we are to be patient while God works. We are not hopeless cases. We can hope in the One who will deliver us in His time.

We now have these two assurances: God's unfailing love—He will never leave us nor forsake us (Hebrews 13:5). And God's promise of full redemption in due time—He will redeem us from all our iniquities (Psalm 130:8) and present us before His glorious presence without fault and with great joy (Jude 24).

We're forgiven! We're free! With the psalmist, let's worship the Lord as we await His coming.

When we're forgiven,
no record is kept of our failures.

When my heart was grieved
and my spirit embittered,
I was senseless and ignorant;
I was a brute beast before you.
Yet I am always with you;
you hold me by my right hand.
You guide me with your counsel,
and afterward you will take me into glory.
Whom have I in heaven but you?
And earth has nothing I desire besides you.
My flesh and my heart may fail,
but God is the strength of my heart
and my portion forever.
Those who are far from you will perish;
you destroy all who are unfaithful to you.
But as for me, it is good to be near God.
I have made the Sovereign Lord my refuge;
I will tell of all your deeds.

Homecoming

You guide me with your counsel,
and afterward you will take me into glory.
—PSALM 73:24

One of my favorite pastimes as a boy was walking the creek behind our home. Those walks were high adventure for me: rocks to skip, birds to watch, dams to build, animal tracks to follow. And if I made it to the mouth of the creek, my dog and I would sit and share lunch while we watched the biplanes land across the lake.

We'd linger as long as we could, but only so long, for my father wanted me home before sunset. The shadows grew long and the hollows got dark fast in the woods. I'd be wishing along the way that I was already home.

Our house sat on a hill behind some trees, but the light was always on until all the family was in. Often my father would be sitting on the back porch, reading the paper, waiting for me. "How did it go?" he would ask. "Pretty good," I'd say. "But it sure is good to be home."

Those memories of walking that creek make me think of another journey—the one I'm making now. It isn't always easy, but I know at the end of it there's a caring Father and my eternal home. I can hardly wait to get there.

I'm expected there. The light is on and my heavenly Father is waiting for me. I suppose He'll ask, just like my father used to, "How did it go?" "Pretty good," I'll say. "But it sure is good to be Home."

For the Christian,
heaven is spelled H-O-M-E.

Lord, who may dwell in your sacred tent?
Who may live on your holy mountain?
The one whose walk is blameless,
who does what is righteous,
who speaks the truth from their heart;
whose tongue utters no slander,
who does no wrong to a neighbor,
and casts no slur on others;
who despises a vile person
but honors those who fear the Lord;
who keeps an oath even when it hurts,
and does not change their mind;
who lends money to the poor without interest;
who does not accept a bribe against the innocent.
Whoever does these things
will never be shaken.

The Best Question

LORD, who may dwell in your sacred tent?
Who may live on your holy mountain?
—PSALM 15:1

Nobel Prize-winning physicist Martin Perl was asked what he attributed his success to. "My mother," he answered. "Every day when I came home from school she asked me, 'So, Marty, did you ask any good questions today?'"

King David asked the best question of all: "LORD, who may dwell in your sacred tent?" (Psalm 15:1). There are two words ancient Jews had for expressing the question "who?" One is similar to our usage. But David used another word here that asks, "What kind of person dwells close to God?"

The answer came in a series of character traits: "The one whose walk is blameless, who does what is righteous, who speaks the truth from [the] heart" (v. 2).

It's one thing to know the truth; it's another to obey it. God delights to live on His holy hill with those who are holy—who reflect the reality of the truth they believe. He loves men and women who "ring true."

This Psalm, however, is not about any holiness of our own that we think will qualify us to gain entrance to His presence. It is rather about the beauty of holiness that God forms in us as we dwell in fellowship with Him.

The closer we get to God, the more like Him we will become.

**Walk so close to God
that nothing can come between.**

Even in darkness light dawns for the upright,
for those who are gracious and compassionate and righteous.
Good will come to those who are generous and lend freely,
who conduct their affairs with justice.
Surely the righteous will never be shaken;
they will be remembered forever.
They will have no fear of bad news;
their hearts are steadfast, trusting in the LORD.
Their hearts are secure, they will have no fear;
in the end they will look in triumph on their foes.
They have freely scattered their gifts to the poor,
their righteousness endures forever;
their horn will be lifted high in honor.

Righteousness
Endures Forever

His righteousness endures forever.
—PSALM 112:9 (NKJV)

A good deal of our unhappiness as we grow older is caused by our pining for the "good old days"—those times when we enjoyed health, wealth, position, or power. But the things of this world don't last. They are vacillating, changeable, capricious. In time, they may be taken away from us and replaced with poverty, isolation, weakness, and pain.

When we realize that this world and everything in it is unstable and unpredictable, we are left longing for something that lasts. What is left?

The psalmist wrote, "[God's] righteousness endures forever" (112:9). It is untouched and unharmed by time and circumstances. Nothing that happens in this world can take it away. It endures when life has stripped us of every other possession.

This righteousness is ours as we draw near to God through faith in Jesus Christ (see Romans 1:17; 3:21–26). He is our rock and our salvation and the only source of true and lasting happiness. Psalm 112:1 says, "Blessed [happy] are those who fear the LORD, who find great delights in his commands."

Delight in the Lord and in His Word, and you'll find true happiness. He alone offers a righteousness that endures for all eternity.

**Happiness is ours
when we delight in the Lord.**

PSALM 16

Keep me safe, my God,
for in you I take refuge.
I say to the LORD, "You are my Lord;
apart from you I have no good thing."
I say of the holy people who are in the land,
"They are the noble ones in whom is all my delight."
Those who run after other gods will suffer more and more.
I will not pour out libations of blood to such gods
or take up their names on my lips.
LORD, you alone are my portion and my cup;
you make my lot secure.
The boundary lines have fallen for me in pleasant places;
surely I have a delightful inheritance.
I will praise the LORD, who counsels me;
even at night my heart instructs me.
I keep my eyes always on the LORD.
With him at my right hand, I will not be shaken.
Therefore my heart is glad and my tongue rejoices;
my body also will rest secure,
because you will not abandon me to the realm of the dead,
nor will you let your faithful one see decay.
You make known to me the path of life;
you will fill me with joy in your presence,
with eternal pleasures at your right hand.

Sleepless Nights

I will praise the LORD, who counsels me;
even at night my heart instructs me.
—PSALM 16:7

The psalmist David had his dark, lonely nights when everything seemed out of control. Doubts and fears assailed him, and there was no escape from his problems. He tossed and turned just as we do, but then he turned to his Shepherd (Psalm 23:1) and reminded himself of the Lord's presence. That brought peace to his anxious, troubled soul. David said, "With him at my right hand, I will not be shaken" (16:8).

We too have occasions of wakefulness when anxious thoughts jostle one another for attention, when we curse the darkness, and when we long for sleep. But we mustn't fret, for darkness can be our friend. God is present in it, visiting us, counseling us, instructing us in the night. Perhaps on our beds, as nowhere else, we may hear God's voice. We can listen to His thoughts and meditate on His Word.

We can talk to the Lord about every concern, casting our care on Him (1 Peter 5:7). We can talk about our failures, our conflicts, our challenges, our anxieties, our frustrations over His lengthy delays—all the things that stress us out and render us sleepless—and listen to what He has to say. That's what can set us apart from ordinary insomniacs. That's the secret of quiet rest.

When you can't sleep, don't count sheep.
Talk to the Shepherd.

PSALM 137:7–8

Remember, LORD, what the Edomites did
on the day Jerusalem fell.
"Tear it down," they cried,
"tear it down to its foundations!"
Daughter Babylon, doomed to destruction,
happy is the one who repays you
according to what you have done to us.

How to Carve a Duck

For those God foreknew
he also predestined to be conformed
to the image of his Son.
—ROMANS 8:29

My wife, Carolyn, and I met Phipps Festus Bourne in 1995 in his shop in Mabry Hill, Virginia. Bourne, who died in 2002, was a master wood carver whose carvings are almost exact replicas of real objects. "Carving a duck is simple," he said. "You just look at a piece of wood, get in your head what a duck looks like, and then cut off everything that doesn't look like it."

So it is with God. He looks at you and me—blocks of rough wood—envisions the Christlike woman or man hidden beneath the bark, knots, and twigs and then begins to carve away everything that does not fit that image. We would be amazed if we could see how beautiful we are as finished "ducks."

But first we must accept that we are a block of wood and allow the Artist to cut, shape, and sand us where He will. This means viewing our circumstances—pleasant or unpleasant—as God's tools that shape us. He forms us, one part at a time, into the beautiful creature He envisioned in our ungainly lump of wood.

Sometimes the process is wonderful; sometimes it is painful. But in the end, all of God's tools conform us "to the image of his Son" (Romans 8:29).

Do you long for that likeness? Put yourself in the Master Carver's hands.

Growing in Christ comes from a deepening relationship with Him.

Praise the LORD, my soul;
all my inmost being, praise his holy name.
Praise the LORD, my soul,
and forget not all his benefits—
who forgives all your sins
and heals all your diseases,
who redeems your life from the pit
and crowns you with love and compassion,
who satisfies your desires with good things
so that your youth is renewed like the eagle's.

Remembering

*Praise the LORD, my soul,
and forget not all his benefits.*
—PSALM 103:2

Some days we awaken with aching joints and dull spirits and wonder how we can shake off our lethargy and make it through the day.

Here's an idea: Like David, try lifting up your thanks to God. Use mind and memory to rekindle thankfulness for all God's "benefits" (Psalm 103:2). Gratefulness will lead to joy.

Thank God for His forgiveness. He "forgives all your sins" (v. 3), and hurled "all our iniquities into the depths of the sea" (Micah 7:19).

Thank Him for healing your diseases (Psalm 103:3). God uses infirmity and disorders to draw you more deeply into His love and care. And, one day when your Lord comes for you, He will heal all of your diseases.

Thank Him for redeeming your life from destruction (v. 4). This is more than rescue from a premature death. It is redemption from death itself.

Thank Him for crowning your life "with love and compassion" (v. 4).

Thank the One who satisfies your desires (v. 5). He is your satisfaction. Each day, He renews your strength and vigor. Then your spirit can rise up and soar like the eagle.

"Praise the LORD, my soul, and forget not all his benefits" (v. 2).

**Gratitude is the memory
of a glad heart.**

Praise the LORD.
Blessed are those who fear the LORD,
who find great delight in his commands.
Their children will be mighty in the land;
the generation of the upright will be blessed.
Wealth and riches are in their houses,
and their righteousness endures forever.
Even in darkness light dawns for the upright,
for those who are gracious and compassionate and righteous.
Good will come to those who are generous and lend freely,
who conduct their affairs with justice.
Surely the righteous will never be shaken;
they will be remembered forever.
They will have no fear of bad news;
their hearts are steadfast, trusting in the LORD.
Their hearts are secure, they will have no fear;
in the end they will look in triumph on their foes.
They have freely scattered their gifts to the poor,
their righteousness endures forever;
their horn will be lifted high in honor.
The wicked will see and be vexed,
they will gnash their teeth and waste away;
the longings of the wicked will come to nothing.

The Work of Our Hands

The righteous will never be shaken;
they will be remembered forever.
—PSALM 112:6

One reason we're left here on earth and not taken to heaven immediately after trusting in Christ for salvation is that God has work for us to do. "Man is immortal," Augustine said, "until his work is done."

The time of our death is not determined by anyone or anything here on earth. That decision is made in the councils of heaven. When we have done all that God has in mind for us to do, then and only then will He take us home—and not one second before. As Paul put it, "when David had served God's purpose in his own generation, he fell asleep" (Acts 13:36).

In the meantime, until God takes us home, there's plenty to do. "I must work the works of Him who sent Me while it is day," Jesus said. "Night is coming, when no one can work" (John 9:4 NKJV). Night is coming when we will once for all close our eyes on this world, or our Lord will return to take us to be with Him. Each day brings that time a little closer.

As long as we have the light of day, we must work—not to conquer, acquire, accumulate, and retire, but to make visible the invisible Christ by touching people with His love. We can then be confident that our "labor in the Lord is not in vain" (1 Corinthians 15:58).

**In God's eyes,
true greatness is serving others.**

PSALM 93

The LORD reigns, he is robed in majesty;
the LORD is robed in majesty and armed with strength;
indeed, the world is established, firm and secure.
Your throne was established long ago;
you are from all eternity.
The seas have lifted up, LORD,
the seas have lifted up their voice;
the seas have lifted up their pounding waves.
Mightier than the thunder of the great waters,
mightier than the breakers of the sea—
the LORD on high is mighty.
Your statutes, LORD, stand firm;
holiness adorns your house
for endless days.

Angry Floods

The seas have lifted up, LORD,
the seas have lifted up their voice;
the seas have lifted up their pounding waves.
—PSALM 93:3

Trouble comes our way, according to Psalm 93, in relentless waves that surge and pound against our souls and break upon them with furious force. "The seas have lifted up, LORD, the seas have lifted up their voice," and they are deafening (v. 3).

Yet above the tempest we hear the psalmist's refrain: "Mightier than the thunder of the great waters, mightier than the breakers of the sea—the LORD on high is mighty" (v. 4).

Indeed, the Lord reigns! He is clothed with majesty and strength. He sits as King, exalted higher than the waves that rise above us, deeper than their immeasurable depths, greater than their strongest surge. The storm is in His all-powerful hands: "The world is established, so that it cannot be moved," for His rule over it was established long ago (v. 1 NKJV). He rules the raging of the sea; the "wind and the waves obey him" (Mark 4:37–41). He speaks and they are still.

The storm will not last forever. Yet, while it rages, you can cling to the Lord's promises of love and faithfulness, for His "statutes . . . stand firm" (Psalm 93:5). Waves of trouble and grief may sweep over you, but you will not be swept away. He "is able to keep you from stumbling" (Jude 24). Our Father in heaven is holding your hand.

When adversity is ready to strike us,
then God is most ready to strengthen us.

God is renowned in Judah;
in Israel his name is great.
His tent is in Salem,
his dwelling place in Zion.
There he broke the flashing arrows,
the shields and the swords, the weapons of war.
You are radiant with light,
more majestic than mountains rich with game.
The valiant lie plundered,
they sleep their last sleep;
not one of the warriors
can lift his hands.
At your rebuke, God of Jacob,
both horse and chariot lie still.
It is you alone who are to be feared.
Who can stand before you when you are angry?
From heaven you pronounced judgment,
and the land feared and was quiet—
when you, God, rose up to judge,
to save all the afflicted of the land.
Surely your wrath against mankind brings you praise,
and the survivors of your wrath are restrained.
Make vows to the Lord your God and fulfill them;
let all the neighboring lands
bring gifts to the One to be feared.
He breaks the spirit of rulers;
he is feared by the kings of the earth.

God's Restraint

Surely your wrath against mankind brings you praise,
and the survivors of your wrath are restrained.
—PSALM 76:10

Augustine said that God "judged it better to bring good out of evil, than not to permit any evil to exist." Thus God takes the worst evil that men and women can do to us and turns it into good. Even the wrath of ungodly men brings praise to Him (Psalm 76:10).

God has not promised that your life will be easy—indeed it may not be. But He has promised to sustain you in your struggle and uphold you with His mighty arm. If you trust Him, He will empower you to make your way bravely through extraordinary difficulty with faith, hope, and love. The trials God permits in your life will lead to His praise and glory, if only you will abide in Him.

Furthermore, there will be a restraint and a respite. The Hebrew text is somewhat obscure in Psalm 76:10. Literally it reads, "Surely the wrath of man will praise You; the remnant of wrath [God] will bind." God will use men's wrath to bring glory and praise to himself, but when that purpose is fulfilled He will then restrain it.

God will not allow you to be pressed beyond endurance. That is His sure promise. When the lesson has been learned, when the revelation of God's glory is complete and your soul has been tried and proven—then God will raise His hand and save you. He will say, "No more."

In every desert of trial,
God provides an oasis of comfort.

Give thanks to the LORD, for he is good.
His love endures forever.
Give thanks to the God of gods.
His love endures forever.
Give thanks to the Lord of lords:
His love endures forever.
to him who alone does great wonders,
His love endures forever.
who by his understanding made the heavens,
His love endures forever.
who spread out the earth upon the waters,
His love endures forever.
who made the great lights—
His love endures forever.
the sun to govern the day,
His love endures forever.
the moon and stars to govern the night;
His love endures forever.

Begin Where You Are

The heavens declare the glory of God;
the skies proclaim the work of his hands.
—PSALM 19:1

I came across a solitary flower growing in a meadow today—a tiny purple blossom "wasting its sweetness in the desert air," to borrow from the poet Thomas Gray's wonderful line. I'm sure no one had seen this particular flower before, and perhaps no one will see it again. Why this beauty in this place? I thought.

Nature is never wasted. It daily displays the truth, goodness, and beauty of the One who brought it into being. Every day, nature offers a new and fresh declaration of God's glory. Do I see Him through that beauty, or do I merely glance at it and shrug it off in indifference?

All nature declares the beauty of the One who made it. Our response can be worship, adoration, and thanksgiving—for the radiance of a cornflower, the splendor of a morning sunrise, the symmetry of one particular tree.

Author C. S. Lewis describes a walk in the forest on a hot summer day. He had just asked his friend how best to cultivate a heart thankful toward God. His hiking companion turned to a nearby brook, splashed his face and hands in a little waterfall, and asked, "Why not begin with this?" Lewis said he learned a great principle in that moment: "Begin where you are."

A trickling waterfall, the wind in the willows, a baby robin, the blue sky, a tiny flower. Why not begin your thankfulness with this?

> **[God] is the beauty behind all beauty.**
> —STEVE DEWITT

I love you, Lᴏʀᴅ, my strength.
The Lᴏʀᴅ is my rock, my fortress and my deliverer;
my God is my rock, in whom I take refuge,
my shield and the horn of my salvation, my stronghold.
I called to the Lᴏʀᴅ, who is worthy of praise,
and I have been saved from my enemies.

The Lord Is My Rock

The LORD is my rock,
my fortress and my deliverer;
my God is my rock, in whom I take refuge,
my shield and the horn of my salvation.
—PSALM 18:2

It turns out that we humans reason largely by means of our hearts and not by our heads. As French mathematician and theologian Blaise Pascal noted long ago, "The heart has reasons that reason does not know."

Poets, singers, storytellers, and artists have always known this. They use symbols and metaphors that speak to our hearts rather than to our minds. That's why their ideas penetrate where everything else has failed. And that's why we say, "A picture is worth a thousand words." Images remain in our minds when all else is forgotten.

David wrote, "The LORD is my rock and my fortress, . . . my shield and the horn of my salvation, my stronghold" (Psalm 18:2 NKJV). He was thinking of physical elements that convey spiritual realities. Each picture expresses a deeper thought, linking the visible world to the invisible realm of the Spirit. David doesn't wander into definition and explanation, for explanation can blunt imagination. Each picture is left hanging in our minds—images that evoke mystery, arouse our imagination, and deepen our understanding.

David wakes up what is hidden deep within us. It's good to think long thoughts about it. What does this mean to you: God is my rock, my fortress, my shield?

Faith bridges chasms
that reason cannot fathom.

How many are your works, Lord!
In wisdom you made them all;
the earth is full of your creatures.
There is the sea, vast and spacious,
teeming with creatures beyond number—
living things both large and small.
There the ships go to and fro,
and Leviathan, which you formed to frolic there.
All creatures look to you
to give them their food at the proper time.
When you give it to them,
they gather it up;
when you open your hand,
they are satisfied with good things.
When you hide your face,
they are terrified;
when you take away their breath,
they die and return to the dust.
When you send your Spirit,
they are created,
and you renew the face of the ground.
May the glory of the Lord endure forever;
may the Lord rejoice in his works—
he who looks at the earth, and it trembles,
who touches the mountains, and they smoke.
I will sing to the Lord all my life;
I will sing praise to my God as long as I live.
May my meditation be pleasing to him,
as I rejoice in the Lord.
But may sinners vanish from the earth
and the wicked be no more.

Bird Song

I will establish your line forever
and make your throne firm
through all generations.
—PSALM 89:4

Why do birds sing? Birds sing "because they can and because they must," says David Rothenberg, a professor at the New Jersey Institute of Technology. "Songs are used to attract mates and defend territories, but the form is much more than function. Nature is full of beauty, and of music."

Birds sing because they have a syrinx instead of a larynx. The syrinx is the bird's voice box, an organ that lies deep in a bird's chest and is uniquely fashioned for song. That, at least, is the natural explanation for their gift.

But I ask again, why do birds sing? Because their Creator put a song in their hearts. Each bird is "heaven's high and holy muse," said John Donne, created to draw our hearts up to our Creator. They are reminders that He has given us a song that we may sing His praise.

So when you hear God's little hymn-birds singing their hearts out, remember to sing your own song of salvation. Lift up your voice—harmonious, hoarse, or harsh—and join with them in praise to our Creator, Redeemer, and Lord.

The birds of the air "sing among the branches," Israel's poet observes (Psalm 104:12). "[Therefore] I will sing to the LORD all my life; I will sing praise to my God as long as I live" (v. 33).

All creation sings
God's praise.

When the LORD restored the fortunes of Zion,
we were like those who dreamed.
Our mouths were filled with laughter,
our tongues with songs of joy.
Then it was said among the nations,
"The LORD has done great things for them."
The LORD has done great things for us,
and we are filled with joy.

Making Melody

Speaking to one another with psalms,
hymns, and songs from the Spirit.
—EPHESIANS 5:19

Do you know why bees hum? It's because they can't remember the words!

Ironically, that old joke reminds me of a serious story I read about a man awaiting heart bypass surgery. He was aware that people die during surgery. As he thought about all that could go wrong, he felt very much alone.

Then an orderly walked into his room to take him to surgery. As the young man began to push his gurney along the corridor, the patient heard him humming an ancient Irish hymn, "Be Thou My Vision." It prompted his memories of lush green fields and the ancient stone ruins of Ireland, the land of his birth. The hymn flooded his soul like a fresh breath of home. When the orderly finished with that song, he hummed Horatio Spafford's hymn, "It Is Well With My Soul."

When they stopped outside the surgical suite, the man thanked him for the hymns. "God has used you this day," he said, "to remove my fears and restore my soul." "How so?" the orderly asked in surprise. "Your 'hums' brought God to me," the man replied.

"The LORD has done great things for us" (Psalm 126:3). He has filled our heart with song. He may even use our "hums" to restore someone's soul.

**Praise flows freely from
the choir of the redeemed.**

I will extol the LORD at all times;
his praise will always be on my lips.
I will glory in the LORD;
let the afflicted hear and rejoice.
Glorify the LORD with me;
let us exalt his name together.
I sought the LORD, and he answered me;
he delivered me from all my fears.
Those who look to him are radiant;
their faces are never covered with shame.
This poor man called, and the LORD heard him;
he saved him out of all his troubles.
The angel of the LORD encamps around those who fear him,
and he delivers them.

Seeing the Unseen

*The angel of the L*ORD *encamps*
around those who fear him,
and he delivers them.
—PSALM 34:7

In a materialistic world like ours, we are tempted to conclude that the only real things are those we experience with our five senses. Yet "there are things we cannot see: things behind our backs or far away and all things in the dark," said C. S. Lewis.

There is another realm of reality, just as actual, just as factual, just as substantial as anything we see, hear, touch, taste, or smell in this world. It exists all around us—not out there "somewhere," but "here." There are legions of angels helping us, for which the world has no counter-measures (Hebrews 1:14). The psalmist David referred to them as a force of thousands of thousands of chariots (Psalm 68:17). We cannot see God nor His angels with our natural eyes. But they are there, whether we see them or not. I believe the world is filled with them.

Faith is the means by which we are able to "see" this invisible world. That is belief's true function. Faith is to the spiritual realm what the five senses are to the natural realm. The writer of Hebrews says that faith is the "assurance about what we do not see" (Hebrews 11:1). By faith we recognize the existence of the spiritual world and learn to depend on the Lord for His help in our daily life. Our goal, then, as George MacDonald once said, is to "grow eyes" to see the unseen.

**Faith sees things
that are out of sight.**

Where can I go from your Spirit?
Where can I flee from your presence?
If I go up to the heavens, you are there;
if I make my bed in the depths, you are there.
If I rise on the wings of the dawn,
if I settle on the far side of the sea,
even there your hand will guide me,
your right hand will hold me fast.
If I say, "Surely the darkness will hide me
and the light become night around me,"
even the darkness will not be dark to you;
the night will shine like the day,
for darkness is as light to you.
For you created my inmost being;
you knit me together in my mother's womb.
I praise you because I am fearfully and wonderfully made;
your works are wonderful,
I know that full well.
My frame was not hidden from you
when I was made in the secret place,
when I was woven together in the depths of the earth.
Your eyes saw my unformed body;
all the days ordained for me were written in your book
before one of them came to be.

Wonderfully Made

*I praise you because I am fearfully
and wonderfully made.*
—PSALM 139:14

A quote in George MacDonald's book *David Elginbrod* speaks to those who sometimes wonder why God has made them the way they are—and who wish they were someone else.

Lady Emily muses: "I wish I were you, Margaret."

Margaret answers: "If I were you, my lady, I would rather be what God chose to make me than the most glorious creature that I could think of. For to have been thought about—born in God's thoughts—and then made by God, is the dearest, grandest, most precious thing in all thinking."

MacDonald may have had Psalm 139:17 in mind: "How precious . . . are your thoughts, God!" In this Psalm, David is thinking about his conception, and he vividly describes God's thoughts as He wove him together in his mother's womb, creating a unique and special individual to be the object of His love.

It's a comforting thought to know that we're not a terrible mistake but a very special creation, "born in God's thoughts." David could stand before a mirror and say in all honesty and humility: "I am fearfully and wonderfully made; your works are wonderful" (v. 14).

You are a designer original! As such, you are dear, grand, and precious to God.

**You are one of a kind—
designed to glorify God as only you can.**

PSALM 34:4–8

I sought the Lord, and he answered me;
he delivered me from all my fears.
Those who look to him are radiant;
their faces are never covered with shame.
This poor man called, and the Lord heard him;
he saved him out of all his troubles.
The angel of the Lord encamps around those who fear him,
and he delivers them.
Taste and see that the Lord is good;
blessed is the one who takes refuge in him.

The Hiding Place

Taste and see that the LORD is good;
blessed is the one who takes refuge in him.
—PSALM 34:8

In this world's misery there is only one sure refuge: God himself. "He shields all who take refuge in him" (Psalm 18:30).

The Hebrew word *chacah* at the end of this verse means "to take refuge in" or "to hide in" or "to hide with." It suggests a secret place of concealment—a "hidey hole," as we used to say when I was growing up in Texas.

When we're exhausted by our efforts, when we're bewildered by our problems, when we're wounded by our friends, when we're surrounded by our foes, we can hide ourselves in God. There is no safety in this world. If we were to find safety here, we would never know the joy of God's love and protection. We would miss the happiness for which we were made.

The only safe place is God himself. When storm clouds gather and calamities loom, we must run into His presence in prayer and remain there (Psalm 57:1).

George MacDonald said, "That man is perfect in faith who can come to God in the utter dearth of his feelings and desires, without a glow or an aspiration, with the weight of low thoughts, failures, neglects, and wandering forgetfulness, and say to Him, 'Thou art my refuge.'"

How safe and blessed we are!

Safety is not found in the absence of danger
but in the presence of God.

PSALM 70

Hasten, O God, to save me;
come quickly, Lord, to help me.
May those who want to take my life
be put to shame and confusion;
may all who desire my ruin
be turned back in disgrace.
May those who say to me, "Aha! Aha!"
turn back because of their shame.
But may all who seek you
rejoice and be glad in you;
may those who long for your saving help always say,
"The Lord is great!"
But as for me, I am poor and needy;
come quickly to me, O God.
You are my help and my deliverer;
Lord, do not delay.

Waiting

Make haste to help me, O LORD!
—PSALM 70:1 (NKJV)

"Make haste to help me, O LORD!" the psalmist David prayed (Psalm 70:1 NKJV). Like him, we don't like to wait. We dislike the long lines at supermarket checkout counters, and the traffic jams downtown and around shopping malls. We hate to wait at the bank or at a restaurant.

And then there are the harder waits: a childless couple waiting for a child; a single person waiting for marriage; an addict waiting for deliverance; a spouse waiting for a kind and gentle word; a worried patient waiting for a diagnosis from a doctor.

What we wait for, however, is far less important than what God is doing while we wait. In such times He works in us to develop those hard-to-achieve spiritual virtues of meekness, kindness, and patience with others. But more important, we learn to lean on God alone and to "rejoice and be glad" in Him (v. 4).

F. B. Meyer said, "What a chapter might be written of God's delays! It is the mystery of the art of educating human spirits to the finest temper of which they are capable. What searchings of heart, what analyzings of motives, what testings of the Word of God, what upliftings of soul. . . . All these are associated with those weary days of waiting, which are, nevertheless, big with spiritual destiny."

**God stretches our patience
to enlarge our soul.**

Help us get the word out!

Our Daily Bread Publishing exists to feed the soul with the Word of God.

If you appreciated this book, please let others know.

- Pick up another copy to give as a gift.
- Share a link to the book or mention it on social media.
- Write a review on your blog, on a bookseller's website, or at our own site (ourdailybreadpublishing.org).
- Recommend this book for your church, book club, or small group.

Connect with us:

 @ourdailybread

 @ourdailybread

 @ourdailybread

Our Daily Bread Publishing
PO Box 3566
Grand Rapids, Michigan 49501 USA

 books@odb.org